30 Second Devotional

30 Second Devotional

Barry Young

Scripture quotations taken from The Holy Bible, New International Version®
NIV®
Copyright © 1973, 1978, 1984, 2011 by Biblica, Inc.™
Used by permission. All rights reserved worldwide.

ISBN-13: 9781545126363
ISBN-10: 1545126364
Library of Congress Control Number: 2017905254
CreateSpace Independent Publishing Platform
North Charleston, South Carolina

Dedication

This book is dedicated to the best part of my life, my beloved wife, Kelly. Although I have just completed a book with thousands of words, phrases, and sentences, I could never adequately communicate to you how thankful I am that you love me.

Acknowledgment

§

I WANT TO SAY I deeply love and appreciate these incredible people below for their support, wisdom, and godly direction. Without them, Serving Pastors Ministries would have never started!

Steve and Jane Faries. Words cannot thank you enough! Your wisdom has proved to be completely invaluable. I am extremely thankful for the weekend that changed my life in Ellijay, Georgia. I love you.

Sue Young and Karen Faries. I don't know how a man could have a better mother and mother-in-law. I am so extremely thankful and blessed to have both of you in my life. I deeply love you.

Dr. Ray Brewer. Pastor, I love you and appreciate you being a spiritual father to me. You will never understand and know the impact you have had on my family and me this side of heaven.

Vaughn Baker. Brother, every time I see you I am completely amazed at how God has used and is using you to save people's lives. Thank you for allowing me to work with you.

Pastor Brad Oyler. I am so extremely thankful for the divine appointments we have had over and over. You were the very first person who saw and spoke dreams over me that I just couldn't see. Brother, I view you and love you as if your last name were Young.

Facts About Your Life

§

SCIENCE CAN'T ANSWER THE THREE most important questions we have in life. Where did we come from? Why are we here? Where will we go when we die?

Friend, it isn't an accident that this book is in your hand. One day you are going to die, and so will I. Are you walking with God? Are you right with God? Have you asked his Son, Jesus Christ, into your life? There is absolutely no way you, by yourself, can earn eternal life! The Bible clearly states in Romans 3:23, "All have sinned." The Bible also clearly states in Romans 6:23, "For the wages of sin is death." We will all die, and if we do not receive the gift of eternal life found only in Jesus, we have nothing to look forward to but physical death and then an eternity separated from God. There is, however, hope!

PRAYER OF SALVATION

Having eternal life with God is not about a religion; it is not about a specific church, and it is certainly not about the efforts of man. Having eternal life is about a person, Jesus Christ.

If you would like to receive Jesus Christ as Lord, he can save you, forgive you, heal you, love you, and most importantly, give you eternal life. The Bible says in Romans 10:9-10, "If you declare with your mouth, 'Jesus is Lord,' and believe in your heart that God raised him from the dead, you will be saved. For it is with your heart that you believe and are justified, and it is with your mouth that you profess your faith and are saved." If you would like to receive eternal life, would you pray this prayer?

Lord Jesus, right now I call on your name. I ask you to be the Lord of my life. I ask you to forgive me for all of my sins. I confess with my mouth and I believe in my heart that you died on the cross and rose from the grave. I receive your love and your salvation.

Friend, if you prayed that prayer in faith, you are now a Christian. If you are not in a Bible-believing church, start attending one now. As believers, we need one another. If you prayed this prayer, would you contact our ministry at www.servingpastors.com? We would love to hear your story.

Introduction

§

I AM SO GLAD YOU are holding this book in your hand. If you are reading this book, just know I have prayed for you. I have prayed that God would use this book to bless, empower, and encourage every reader to live a totally sold-out life of adventure and favor for Jesus.

The goal of this book is not for people to spend 30 seconds with God and stop. No, quite the contrary. Statistics tell us the overwhelming majority of Christians do not spend daily time with God. Oftentimes, spending daily time with God is referred to as a quiet time or devotional time. The key to believers having blessed lives, forming healthy relationships, and becoming all that God wants them to be simply rests in spending daily time with God!

The goal of this book is to get every reader spending daily time with God. Thirty seconds a day with God isn't the finish line; it is the starting line. Listen to this scripture from Psalm 34:8, "Taste and see that the Lord is good; blessed is the one who takes refuge in him." My goal is for readers of this book to taste and see that the Lord is good and want more of him.

I believe if you will start spending 30 seconds with God daily for an entire year, then the goodness of God will overwhelm you. The more time you spend with God, the more you will want to meet with him. I believe 30 seconds with God can turn into a daily intimate meeting between a loving heavenly Father and his child. I believe that daily intimate meetings will turn into a life full of God's promises fulfilled and amazing adventures lived.

God has amazing plans for your life! God wants to do more in your life than you can imagine. In John 10:10 Jesus said, "I have come that they may have life, and have it to the full." The only way to have abundant life is to spend daily time with the author of life. God loves you, and so do I. Be blessed!

Barry

JANUARY 1ST

John 14:12—"Very truly I tell you, whoever believes in me will do the work I have been doing, and they will do even greater things than these."

Wow! Did you read that verse? For this upcoming year, God wants to do more in your life than you can believe. In this one verse Jesus says, "they will do even greater things than these." Jesus not only says you can do what he did, but you can do even greater things! We serve an amazing God!

THE TAKEAWAY: Today, start having faith in God to do the thing or things you don't believe you can do.

JANUARY 2ND

2 Corinthians 2:7—"You ought to forgive and comfort him, so that he will not be overwhelmed by excessive sorrow."

We all need someone in our life who will pick us up when we have messed up. No price can repay a friend who steps into our life when everything has gone sideways. Do you know how you get great friends? There is an old saying, "If you want a friend, be a friend." I want to inspire you to look for people in your sphere of life and try to encourage them today. Someday, you will need to be encouraged. Sow encouragement in others today.

THE TAKEAWAY: Do you realize right now people are praying that someone like you would help them out?

JANUARY 3RD

2 Corinthians 10:17—"Let the one who boasts boast in the Lord."

Don't get stuck in the rut of being negative all the time. It is easy to argue, whine, and complain about the difficulties of life. Friend, when you are negative all the time, I promise that you will have fewer friends. However, the main reason we shouldn't speak negatively is we start to believe what we are saying. Today, I want to encourage you to let the goodness of God filter what you say. Sure, you might have problems, but there isn't a problem you struggle with where God doesn't have an answer.

THE TAKEAWAY: Instead of telling God how big your problems are, would you start telling your problems how big your God is?

JANUARY 4TH

Philippians 3:13—"But one thing I do: Forgetting what is behind."

One problem many people struggle with is the habit of focusing on the past. It seems as though we tend to remember our past failures and sins, which then causes us to forfeit enjoying the present. However, it is also just as dangerous to be overwhelmingly focused on your past successes and then to rest on those accomplishments and miss out on the adventure that God has for you today. I want to encourage you to learn from the past. Your past is a point of reference, not a place of residence.

THE TAKEAWAY: Identify what you are struggling with from your past and find out from the Bible what God says about that issue. Every time you are tempted to revisit the past, just remember what God says.

JANUARY 5TH

Genesis 1:31—"God saw all that he made, and it was very good."

Friend, God doesn't make junk. God created you, and he was pleased. As you go through your busy day, you can have 100% confidence that God is for you. If you are tempted to believe that you and your life are not important, you couldn't be more incorrect. If you are tempted to believe that your life must have limitations, you are mistaken. God loves and believes in you, and he can't be wrong.

THE TAKEAWAY: How can you align your thinking with God's perspective?

JANUARY 6TH

Galatians 4:7—"So you are no longer a slave, but God's child."

Sometimes, people struggle in life because they have the wrong picture of God. They might think God is sitting in heaven waiting to strike us with lightning bolts every time we make a mistake. Or, as the above verse mentions, some people think we are God's slaves. However, both pictures are inaccurate. For those who have put their faith in Christ, you are not a slave, but a son or daughter of God's. No matter how many times I have messed up, I am still the son of my dad, Tom Young. And just because you are not perfect and make mistakes at times, doesn't mean you are no longer a son or daughter of God. Be blessed, and don't forget you are a King's kid!

THE TAKEAWAY: It is not only important to remember who you are; it is important to remember whose you are.

JANUARY 7TH

Matthew 19:26—"With God all things are possible."

The truth is that with God there are no limits. And with man there are limits. If you believe you will fail, you will. If you believe you will not make it, you won't. However, if you put your faith in God, no matter how big the obstacle, you can have victory. You have a choice today; you can feed your faith or you can doubt your doubts.

THE TAKEAWAY: The key to victory in life is simply to answer this question: Will you believe God or will you believe your feelings?

JANUARY 8TH

Galatians 6:7—"A man reaps what he sows."

If you want love, give love. If you want forgiveness, forgive those who have wronged you. If you want appreciation, appreciate those in your sphere of influence. If you want to be treated well, treat others well. Friend, God's principle of sowing and reaping is simple: you will reap what you sow. Sow wisely today!

THE TAKEAWAY: Where does God want you to sow seeds of faith today?

JANUARY 9TH

Genesis 1:1—"In the beginning God created the heavens and the earth."

God's love and power know no limits. God has never seen a marriage he couldn't restore, a life he couldn't turn around, a pain he couldn't heal, a soul he didn't love, or a situation he couldn't fix. And God has never seen a problem he doesn't have an answer for. You should be excited about life because no matter where you are, God has what you need.

THE TAKEAWAY: Start looking at your struggles through the lens of God's unlimited power.

JANUARY 10TH

Psalm 126:2—"The Lord has done great things for them."

Everything that is good in your life comes from God. We get into big trouble when we start thinking that we are blessed because of what our hands have done. Sure, you might have worked hard or attended college, but you were able to work hard because God gave you life, and you were able to learn in school because God gave you knowledge and comprehension. Friend, every blessing in your life comes from God. The more we turn to him, the more we get blessed. Always remember, "the Lord has done great things."

THE TAKEAWAY: Take time today to write down the top five things you are thankful for in your life.

JANUARY 11TH

Ephesians 5:16—"Making the most of every opportunity."

Today, you have the opportunity to focus on the positives in your life. Today, you have the opportunity to encourage your coworkers. Today, you have the opportunity to make sure your family knows you love them. Today, you have the opportunity to do something you have never done. Today, you have the opportunity to believe God for something greater for your life. Don't waste today! Make the most out of the opportunities God gives you today.

THE TAKEAWAY: What is it you have wanted to do but haven't done yet? Start it today!

JANUARY 12TH

Psalm 130:3—"If you, Lord, kept a record of sins, Lord, who could stand?"

Why are you keeping a record of mistakes that God isn't keeping a record of? The Bible clearly teaches that if we confess our sins to God, such as in 1 John 1:9, he will forgive us. However, God not only forgives our sins, but he completely wipes our slate clean. Friend, if God isn't thinking about or keeping a record of our sins and mistakes, we shouldn't either! Isn't that good news?

THE TAKEAWAY: Stop remembering what God has forgotten. Too many times we remember what God forgets and we forget what God remembers.

JANUARY 13TH

Philippians 3:10—"I want to know Christ—yes, to know the power of his resurrection."

Where do you need power today? Do you need power to get up to go to work, power to lose weight, power not to give up on a relationship, or power just to make it through a day? Friend, wherever you need power, I have good news for you. God has it! If Jesus can overcome death, hell, and the grave, he can help you overcome any area of your life and give you power in your daily walk!

THE TAKEAWAY: You were created not to be overcome, but to be an overcomer.

JANUARY 14TH

John 11:35—"Jesus wept."

How many times have we heard the phrase, "God loves you"? What I love about this verse is it shows the compassion God has for us, and how much God loves us. When we cry, those tears are proof that we love someone. Friend, the tears of Jesus are one of the many pieces of evidence that he loves you. You are the beloved of God!

THE TAKEAWAY: People don't care how much you know until they know how much you care. Jesus not only tells us of his love, but he demonstrates his love and compassion with his own tears. We need to demonstrate God's love to others.

JANUARY 15TH

Proverbs 30:33—"So stirring up anger produces strife."

Either anger will control you or you will control anger. Here are three things to think about when you are angry:

1) Consider what you will lose when you lose your temper. Sometimes we say words we regret or we lose the respect of others.
2) Gratitude Exercise: When you are angry, focus on the blessings you have in life.
3) Don't make things worse: When you give into anger, things will only go from bad to worse.

THE TAKEAWAY: Will you feed your anger or starve it?

JANUARY 16TH

Colossians 3:15—"Let the peace of Christ rule in your hearts."

How is your heart today? Are you angry, depressed, sad, or maybe excited? In order to have peace in your life, you must "let" the peace of Christ rule in your hearts. If you are filling your heart with junk, you are not "letting" God have his way in your life. If you're allowing your heart to be polluted by outside negative forces, you will never have peace. What we put in our hearts will always come out. There is an old phrase, "garbage in, garbage out."

THE TAKEAWAY: You must be vigilant about monitoring what you let into your mind and life.

JANUARY 17TH

Psalm 121:1—"I lift up my eyes to the mountains—where does my help come from?"

Look up! Lift up your eyes and get them off of the problems or trials you are facing. We can't deny that we are going to have bad days or trials come our way. But sometimes we can get stuck in a rut by just focusing on our problems. When we dwell on our setbacks, it makes it difficult to overcome the issues of life. If you want to see a difference today, look up! Look up to God who has the solutions and power for your everyday life.

THE TAKEAWAY: What is it in your life that tries to keep you from looking up?

JANUARY 18TH

Romans 8:28—"And we know that in all things God works for the good of those who love him."

Your worst hurt, if given to God, can become your greatest tool to help other people. God never wastes a pain. When we experience hurt, we can either become bitter, or we can give that pain to God and become whole. After we choose to let God heal our hearts, we are then better positioned to help those who are going through trials become victorious as well. You have to make a choice today to be bitter or better. You can be pitiful or powerful, but you can't be both. Choose to be powerful!

THE TAKEAWAY: God wants to take your pain and, in exchange, give you power.

JANUARY 19TH

Psalm 4:8—"In peace I will lie down and sleep."

This verse is easier said than done at times. Let me give you five great reasons why you can go to sleep in peace:

1) There is nothing you can't do (Philippians 4:13).
2) God can turn any setback into a setup for a comeback (Genesis 50:20).
3) God loves you (1 John 3:1).
4) God can remove any guilt you have (1 John 1:9).
5) God can heal any hurt in your life (Psalm 147:3).

THE TAKEAWAY: If God is keeping watch over your life at night, there is no use in both of you being up.

JANUARY 20TH

Matthew 6:27—"Can any one of you by worrying add a single hour to your life?"
Matthew 6:34—"Therefore do not worry about tomorrow."

Stop worrying. It isn't doing any good. Let me give you some wise words from an old hymn written by Ira Stanphill:

I don't know about tomorrow, I just live from day to day,
I don't borrow from its sunshine, for its skies may turn to gray.
I don't worry o'er the future, for I know what Jesus said,
And today I'll walk beside Him, for he knows what is ahead.
Many things about tomorrow, I don't seem to understand;
But I know who holds tomorrow, and I know who holds my hand.

THE TAKEAWAY: Worrying can't change our lives, but trusting God can.

JANUARY 21ST

Joshua 1:9—"Be strong and courageous…for the Lord your God will be with you wherever you go."

God doesn't want you to be a weakling. He wants your life to be filled with power! However, if God wants for us to be strong and courageous, why do so many people seem to have so little power in their marriages, finances, dreams, and careers? The reason is too many times we do things without God. We don't consult him, and we don't ask him to be our leader. Friend, alone you will be defeated every time. But when you partner with God, you are powerful and will have the strength and courage you need.

THE TAKEAWAY: You don't need to give into fear because God is with you always and will give you the strength you need to overcome.

JANUARY 22ND

Psalm 7:8—"Let the Lord judge the peoples."

The more we judge people, the more problems that will occur in our relationships. It seems as though when we judge people, we always come out on the losing end. We need to come to the conclusion that the more we take our eyes off of people and put our eyes on God, the more blessed we will be. I want to encourage you to love and pray for the people you disagree with, but don't judge them. Focus on being the best you can be, and let God take care of the rest.

THE TAKEAWAY: When we start judging people, we have taken a turn down the wrong road.

JANUARY 23RD

John 3:16—"For God so loved the world that he gave his one and only Son, that whoever believes in him shall not perish but have eternal life."

A friend of mine asked a young man who had a cross on, "Do you believe in God?" My friend then continued on to say to the young man, "Because God believes in you." As I thought about what my friend said, John 3:16 came to my mind. God believes in us so much that he gave his Son for us so we could have a personal relationship with him. Today, if you are down in the dumps, remember, God believes in you!

THE TAKEAWAY: We can have confidence in life not because of our power, but because of God's.

JANUARY 24TH

1 Corinthians 10:13—"And God is faithful; he will not let you be tempted beyond what you can bear."

Everyone is tempted, but not everyone gives in to temptation. Today, wherever you are tempted, I want you to know, you don't have to give in to that temptation. We are all dealing with something, and friend, God wants you to have his supernatural power. Be blessed, and just know whatever you are going through, God has a way out!

THE TAKEAWAY: Don't try to face your temptation; run from it.

JANUARY 25TH

1 Timothy 3:9—"They must keep hold of the deep truths."

Every day, someone or something will try to steal your joy! Throughout your day, something could happen that will attempt to steal your peace. Friend, I want to encourage you to hold on to the deep truths of God's Word and his promises for your life. God wants to bless your socks off, but you can't let go of his blessing. Whatever tries to steal your victory today, don't give in; instead hold on!

THE TAKEAWAY: Tremendous power builds up in our lives when we simply refuse to quit.

JANUARY 26TH

Ecclesiastes 7:13—"Consider what God has done."

I know there are bad things going on in this world. However, consider how blessed you really are. You are alive. You live in a free country. You are able to follow God with no persecution. You are able to read the words in this book. You are able to pursue life, liberty, and the pursuit of happiness. You are blessed.

THE TAKEAWAY: The more thankful we become, the more powerful we become. The more entitled we become, the weaker we become.

JANUARY 27TH

2 Timothy 1:7—"For the Spirit God gave us does not make us timid, but gives us power, love and self-discipline."

Timid, according to *Webster's Dictionary*, means easily frightened. Friend, God doesn't want you to live in fear; he wants you to live in faith. God doesn't want you to retreat from life but to attack it. If you want an abundant life of favor, peace, and blessing, you cannot be timid about it. People who get defeated in life feed their fear. People that have overwhelming victory in life feed their faith. The choice is up to you.

THE TAKEAWAY: What are you afraid of? Once you have identified your fears, start to lean in toward it.

JANUARY 28TH

Psalm 18:28—"God turns my darkness into light."

I love this verse! Only God can turn the trials, pains, hurts, and junk of life and use those things to bless us. When you look at every problem you face as an opportunity for God to bless you that is when you start living the abundant life.

THE TAKEAWAY: Problems are blessings in work clothes.

JANUARY 29TH

Psalm 20:7—"Some trust in chariots and some in horses, but we trust in the name of the Lord our God."

Who or what are you trusting to get you through life? If you trust something made by man, know that it can break. If your trust is in money made by man, know that it can all be spent. If you are trusting in doctors who practice medicine, know that they can be wrong. If you are trying to get wisdom from a great counselor, know that even they have limits. But if your trust is in God, know that he can't be wrong, he will always be with you, he is perfect in love, and he can create an answer for any problem you have. Trust God.

THE TAKEAWAY: We all have faith! The question is, who or what is our faith in?

JANUARY 30TH

Titus 2:14—"Who gave himself for us to redeem us."

Do you need something in your life turned around? God specializes in doing what we think can't be done. Sometimes the reason we aren't succeeding in life is because we have put self-imposed limits on ourselves, and we don't even realize it. Jesus gave his life so our lives could be redeemed. Give God a chance to turn around the area of your life you are struggling with today.

THE TAKEAWAY: Is there something in your life you need God to make new? Lay your request at the feet of Jesus and watch what he does.

JANUARY 31ST

Isaiah 41:13—"For I am the Lord your God, who takes hold of your right hand and says to you, Do not fear; I will help you."

It doesn't matter whom the president, king, or prime minister is: God is still in control. We need to pray for our nation, but we also need to understand that even presidents have limitations; however, God does not. In this verse, God promises to speak to us and to help us. Wherever you are at today in life, don't be afraid; God wants to hold your hand.

THE TAKEAWAY: Have you really considered the truth that God wants to hold your hand throughout today?

FEBRUARY 1ST

John 10:10—"The thief comes only to steal and kill and destroy; I have come that they may have life, and have it to the full."

Have you ever heard that voice that says, "You can't do it," or "You're not smart enough," or "You will never have that job," or "You will never get married," or "You can never overcome that situation," or "Your life will never be great"? Those negative voices are from the devil. This verse calls him the thief. He wants to steal your joy, peace, and your quality of life. Today, make sure you read the last part of that verse, "That they may have life and have it to the full." Friend, God wants your life full. Today, God wants you to have the life you have always dreamed of but sometimes the only thing standing in the way is you.

THE TAKEAWAY: Will you believe God's truth that nothing is impossible or will you listen to the voices that only say it can never happen? Choose today to have life to the full.

FEBRUARY 2ND

2 Corinthians 6:2—"I tell you, now is the time of God's favor."

What are you waiting on that you should be doing? Should you adopt? Are you supposed to go back to school? Are you supposed to start working on your dream? Friend today is the day of God's favor. Don't put life off; seize today. As followers of Jesus, we are supposed to live life on the offensive.

THE TAKEAWAY: Don't wait to start living your dreams!

FEBRUARY 3RD

Zephaniah 3:17—"The Lord your God is with you, the Mighty Warrior who saves."

God is mighty! He is more powerful than your greatest failure. He is more powerful than your greatest hurt. He is more powerful than any force that can be attacking your life today. He is more powerful than any sickness you might be dealing with. He is more powerful than any negative word that has ever been spoken against you. God is mighty and God is for you.

THE TAKEAWAY: God is bigger than any problem you are facing. As you go through your day, would you remember this truth?

FEBRUARY 4TH

1 John 3:1—"See what great love the Father has lavished on us."

God loves you! God loves you when you fail. God loves you when you succeed. God loves you when you are married. God loves you when you are single. God loves you when you are a parent. God loves you when you are a grandparent. Hey, do you get the message yet? God loves you, and he wants you to know it.

THE TAKEAWAY: Our entire world changes when we understand the revelation that God is overwhelmingly in love with us.

FEBRUARY 5TH

Psalm 34:10—"But those who seek the Lord lack no good thing."

Do you feel as though something is missing from your life? You may not have that certain thing for one of three possible reasons:

1) God doesn't think you should have it. Sometimes, God protects us by not giving us what we want.
2) There is a seeking problem. Sometimes we are lacking because we aren't seeking God.
3) God has something better for you. At times, when we pray, we ask too small, and God wants us to ask bigger!

Friend, God wants you blessed. When you seek his will and submit to him, he will pour out his blessings on you.

THE TAKEAWAY: Contentment is so valuable. Be thankful for what you have.

FEBRUARY 6TH

Hebrews 10:39—"But we do not belong to those who shrink back and are destroyed, but to those who have faith and are saved."

Don't run from your problems; run to them! None of us are fast enough to run away from our problems. But if we run to our problems and face them in the strength and power of God, we will overcome them. When we believe and put our faith in God, even when all heck is breaking loose, he promises to save us.

THE TAKEAWAY: What are you running from? Step out in faith and lean into that issue.

FEBRUARY 7TH

Psalm 108:12—"Give us aid against the enemy, for human help is worthless."

There are times in our lives where no man or woman can help us. There are times where no government or earthly power can meet the need that we may have. Friend, God wants to come to your aid today. Don't let fear, doubt, unbelief, or any earthly force keep you from turning to God. Today, walk in God's strength and power.

THE TAKEAWAY: Where are you trusting man instead of God?

FEBRUARY 8TH

2 Corinthians 5:17—"Therefore, if anyone is in Christ, the new creation has come: The old has gone, the new is here!"

Don't wait to make changes in your life that you have wanted to make. Friend, you can have God's very best in every area of your life. Procrastination is one of the enemies of greatness. Therefore, if you want something changed, change it! If you want something in your life adjusted, adjust it! Tomorrow is not promised.

THE TAKEAWAY: Make a list of your dreams. Then, make a list of steps you will take today to ensure those dreams will come true.

FEBRUARY 9TH

Psalm 41:10—"Raise me up."

This verse is a great prayer we can pray to God. As some of you are reading today's devotional, you are realizing you need to raise up your expectations. God can raise up your dead dreams. God can raise you up from your worst failures. God can raise you out of debt. God can raise you up from plateauing in life to flourishing. God can raise you out of depression. Let God raise you up!

THE TAKEAWAY: If you want God to step into some area of your life and help you, just remember: We have to be part of our own rescue.

FEBRUARY 10TH

Luke 1:37—"For no word from God will ever fail."

Recently a professional football player committed murder and then suicide. However, prior to this incident, he was a man that others looked up to and inspired to be like. Unfortunately, his fame and fortune could not help him with his personal issues. Maybe some really painful stuff is going on inside your life. Let me tell you: you don't have to give up because nothing is impossible with God! This football player isn't the only person the devil has lied to. The devil also tries to lie to all of us on a daily basis. Don't listen to him!

THE TAKEAWAY: Identify where the devil is trying to lie to you. Then find scriptures from the Bible that tell you the truth about that matter.

FEBRUARY 11TH

Philippians 2:5—"In your relationships with one another, have the same mindset as Christ Jesus."

Life can be a blessing if we follow the ABCs of life:

Attitude - If we have a bad attitude, we will have a bad day. If we have a good attitude, we will have a good day.

Behavior - If we sow bad behaviors, we reap bad results. But if we sow good behaviors, we reap good results.

Choices - We can't blame people for our choices. Most of what we face today is a product of our choices. The good news is no matter how bad our choices have been, if we make good choices, things can and will turn around.

THE TAKEAWAY: You can't control others, but you can control you. Live out daily the ABCs of life.

FEBRUARY 12TH

2 Corinthians 6:2—"I tell you, now is the time of God's favor."

Don't spend too much time reading or watching movies about the adventures going on in other people's lives. Focus on living out adventures in your own life. Too many times, we get overly focused on what other people have in their lives. Sometimes, we focus on other people's possessions, and sometimes, we start focusing on other people's adventures. Friend, live out the adventure God has for you!

THE TAKEAWAY: God has an amazing adventure for your life. However, you can never participate in that adventure if your eyes are on someone else's journey.

FEBRUARY 13TH

Joshua 1:5—"I will never leave you nor forsake you."

Wow, this verse is a big promise! We have all made some big mistakes in our lives, but God says he won't leave us. We have committed some unwise sins, but God says he won't leave us. At times, we have made poor choices that have hurt other people, but God says he won't leave us. Friend, anyone can stay with you when the sailing is smooth. But when the seas of life start rocking, God stays with us for the entire ride. What a good God he is!

THE TAKEAWAY: Consider this truth: No matter where you are or what you have done, you cannot outrun the love of God.

FEBRUARY 14TH

1 Corinthians 13:5—"Love keeps no record of wrongs."

As Valentine's Day is upon us, we need to step back and realize this world doesn't really know a lot about love. I'm talking about genuine love. This one phrase is an essential characteristic of love: if you love someone, don't keep a record of the mistakes and sins that person makes. If you want to improve your relationships, stop keeping a log of the negative or hurtful actions. Friend, we know God loves us because he gave love to us through his Son, Jesus. When we are connected to God, he keeps no record of our wrongs.

THE TAKEAWAY: Are you a hurt collector or can you overlook other people's mistakes? I am sure you can guess out of the two types of people who enjoy life more!

FEBRAURY 15TH

Psalm 25:3—"No one who hopes in you will ever be put to shame."

Get your hopes up! Today is a new start and adventure for your life. If someone ever tells you, "Don't get your hopes up," don't listen to them. God wants you to get your hopes up. The Creator of the world wants you to have amazing big dreams. If your hope is in him, you will not be disappointed. I dare you to believe God for something big.

THE TAKEAWAY: Look at the different areas in your life. Where do you need to get your hopes up?

FEBRUARY 16TH

Psalms 66:12—"You brought us to a place of abundance."

God wants you to live in abundance. God doesn't want you to just scrape by in life. He doesn't want your marriage, career, vision, dreams, or life in general just to be mediocre. You can live in abundance, but only when you do things God's way. This year can be a year of abundance for you. Read the Word, speak the Word, and believe the Word!

THE TAKEAWAY: Take a moment to thank God for the areas of your life where he has brought you into abundance. Then begin to believe for his provision in areas where you have need.

FEBRUARY 17TH

Proverbs 3:5-6—"Trust in the Lord with all your heart and lean not on your own understanding; in all your ways submit to him and he will make your paths straight."

Our Part: We are to trust God with everything we hold dear and deem as important. We are to realize we cannot solve every problem we have with our own wisdom and skill.

His Part: God promises that if we will trust him and place our lives in his hands that he will direct, guide, and protect us.

Do your part because God will do his.

THE TAKEAWAY: Is there an area of your life where you have not taken personal responsibility? Step up and own your responsibilities.

FEBRUARY 18TH

Psalm 78:13—"He divided the sea and led them through; he made the water stand up like a wall."

God can make a way for you! Yes, God can get you through that financial hardship. Yes, God can get you through that relationship issue. Yes, God can heal that hurt and pain in your heart. Friend, there is no limit to what God can do. Don't settle, don't waver, and don't throw in the towel.

THE TAKEAWAY: God specializes in doing what we think he can't. Stand on his promises!

FEBRUARY 19TH

2 Timothy 3:16—"All scripture is God-breathed and is useful for teaching, rebuking, correcting and training in righteousness."

God's Word is relevant; it never changes. God's Word doesn't talk about the truth, it is the truth. God's Word doesn't just understand our problems; his Word contains the solutions to our problems. Friend, if you are facing a battle today, find out what God's Word says about that situation, and then stand on that promise, no matter what! If you do, you will be an overcomer in life!

THE TAKEAWAY: Boldly declare God's Word over every area of your life.

FEBRUARY 20TH

Ephesians 3:20—"Now to him who is able to do immeasurably more than all we ask or imagine, according to his power that is at work within us."

Do you have a God-sized dream for your life? God-sized dreams are dreams that are bigger than you. Just think of it; this could be the year you get that degree, start that business, get totally in shape, or you name it. Friend, don't let the devil trick you into settling for a small dream. Ask God for a God-sized dream and then don't let go of it!

THE TAKEAWAY: You know God is speaking to you when he asks you to do something that in your own power you can't do.

FEBRUARY 21ST

Jeremiah 29:11—"For I know the plans I have for you, declares the Lord, plans to prosper you and not to harm you, plans to give you hope and a future."

Life basically comes down to two choices: Our way or God's way. Here are four benefits of doing God's will in our lives:

1) When we do things according to the Bible, we will have no regrets.
2) When we do things God's way, we do them right.
3) When we make godly decisions, we can enjoy those decisions tomorrow.
4) When we do things God's way, we are assured that he will bless what we are doing.

Choose God's will for your life today.

THE TAKEAWAY: Start spending time every day listening for God to speak to you.

FEBRUARY 22ND

Psalm 95:6—"Let us kneel before the Lord our Maker."

There is power when we surrender our lives to God. There is a universal sign that all languages and people groups understand: placing your hands up in the air is the sign for surrender. When we surrender our lives to God, there will be breakthrough where we can see him at work in our lives to bring healing, blessing, and prosperity. If you are struggling in an area of your life today, perhaps there is something you need to surrender to God.

THE TAKEAWAY: Diligently look inside your heart for areas that need to be surrendered to God.

FEBRUARY 23RD

1 Corinthians 15:57—"But thanks be to God! He gives us the victory through our Lord Jesus Christ."

Do you know that you are a champion? Yes, you heard correctly; you are a champion. You're not a champion because I say so or because you say so, no! You are a champion because God says so. If God gives us the victory, then we are champions. My challenge to you today is not to walk around like a defeated, weak, nominal Christian. My challenge for you today is to understand God has made you a champion, and that is what you are!

THE TAKEAWAY: Regardless if you think, feel, or look like a champion; If God says it, how you think and feel is irrelevant.

FEBRUARY 24TH

Colossians 3:1—"Set your hearts on things above."

Get your heart out of mediocre visions. I mean it! God doesn't want you to be focused on small plans for your life, marriage, or career. God wants you to set your heart on things above. Today, God wants to pour down blessings and favor on your life, but he can't do it if your heart is in the wrong place. The more our hearts are focused on the things of God; the more our lives get overwhelmed by his blessings. Make sure you heart is in the right place today.

THE TAKEAWAY: Blessings from God will only flow to hearts that are receptive.

FEBRUARY 25TH

Ephesians 6:18—"Be alert and always keep on praying."

Don't stop praying for that miracle. Don't stop praying for that marriage. Don't stop praying for that financial breakthrough. Don't stop praying for that child or friend to come to Christ. Right now, the devil wants to try to get you to stop praying for that need or concern in your life. Don't stop! You can only be defeated as a son or daughter of God if you stop praying.

THE TAKEAWAY: Prayer moves the hands of God.

FEBRUARY 26TH

John 17:21—"That all of them may be one."

This verse is taken from Jesus's longest prayer in the Bible. The subject of his prayer was the unity of Christians. There is no way that everyone in a church, family, or even marriage can agree on everything. However, we can either be easily offended or we can be hard to offend. We can either be a porcupine person that people are nervous to be around or we can be a life-giving person that people are attracted to. If you sow joy and grace with others, you will reap it. Bring friendship and unity to those around you.

THE TAKEAWAY: Start being someone who is hard to offend and watch how that will change your relationships.

FEBRUARY 27TH

Psalm 108:13—"With God we will gain the victory."

I hate losing! At times, being a sports fan can be painful. However, in life there is a way we can make sure we win, by partnering with God. If you want to ensure you will get defeated, try running your own career, finances, family, without God. God won't force us to do anything. And we don't have to participate with God on anything. But if we want success, the key is to partner with God. Friend, God wants you to have victory in life, but victory only comes when you have a genuine partnership with God.

THE TAKEAWAY: To have God's best, we have to partner with him, not just in name only. Partnering with God means yielding control to him.

FEBRUARY 28TH

Psalm 91:11—"For he will command his angels concerning you."

I am thankful for God's protection! God has protected us from certain incidents where we may have been completely unaware of his intervention. When we make bad choices many times, we are asking God to protect us from ourselves. Today, I want to ask you, are you making life-giving or life-taking choices with your life? You always know you are making a good choice when you can enjoy the choice tomorrow. The worst choices are those we can only enjoy now.

THE TAKEAWAY: A good choice today guarantees a harvest tomorrow.

FEBRUARY 29TH

Psalm 116:15—"Precious in the sight of the Lord is the death of his faithful servants."

Wow! God can bring peace to what we consider the most difficult trial someone can go through...death. Our minds cannot comprehend how great heaven is. Jesus said in John 6:47, "Very truly I tell you, the one who believes has eternal life." When we put our belief or faith in Christ, we are promised everlasting life.

THE TAKEAWAY: For those who are walking with God: Death is not the end, death is the beginning!

MARCH 1ST

John 14:27—"My peace I give you. I do not give to you as the world gives."

God is so good. Look at the two main points of this part of the verse:

1) "My peace I give to you." Wow! Jesus is giving us his peace. His peace that passes all understanding. His peace that when chaos might be all around us, we are still able to remain calm.
2) "I do not give as the world gives." In this world, typically if something is free, it may be worthless in the first place. Or if it is free, it is a gift given with a hidden motive. But not with Jesus. He gives us his peace free of charge. We get this peace just because he loves us.

THE TAKEAWAY: Don't make things harder than they already are. Rise up and refuse to walk in anything but God's peace.

MARCH 2ND

Psalm 124:8—"Our help is in the name of the Lord, the Maker of heaven and earth."

I recently plugged my laptop into an outlet waiting for it to get recharged, but then realized nothing happened. What was the problem? I was plugged into a powerless power source. Friend that can happen to us from time to time. When trials come, we may talk to friends or turn to self-help books, but those resources are sometimes powerless to help us through our trial. I am not saying that talking with friends or reading books is harmful, but they aren't perfect. However, God is the ultimate power source, and when we turn to him, he has the power we need to get through any trial we might be facing.

THE TAKEAWAY: Examine the power sources your life is plugged into. Is there something or someone you need to unplug from?

MARCH 3ND

Psalm 125:2—"The Lord surrounds his people both now and forevermore."

Have you ever been looking for something and you didn't realize it was right in front of you? In Missouri, oftentimes we say, "If it was a snake, it would have bit you." There are times when we go through trials and start to experience pain, and then we assume God isn't with us. However, God doesn't promise to remove the pain of our difficult trials, but he does promise to be with us and help us through our hardships. If you're struggling today, I have a sneaky feeling that if you look hard enough, you might find that God is at work in your life, even in the trials!

THE TAKEAWAY: Don't ask God to remove your trials, but instead ask God to help you go through your trials.

MARCH 4TH

Jeremiah 29:11—"For I know the plans I have for you declares the Lord. Plans to prosper you and not to harm you, plans to give you hope and a future."

Are you walking in God's plans or your own plans for your life? One of the ways we can make God laugh is by telling him our own plans. Here are some words associated with doing things our own way: pain, worry, fear, disappointment, despair. Here are some words associated with doing God's plans for our life: joy, peace, hope, anticipation, and fulfillment. Friend, if you want an unbelievable life, seek God's plan for your life and do it!

THE TAKEAWAY: Take a deep look inside your heart and life, and ask the Holy Spirit if there are any areas of your life where you are doing things your own way instead of his.

MARCH 5TH

Philippians 4:19—"And my God will meet all your needs according to the riches of his glory in Christ Jesus."

We all have a lot of needs, don't we? One trap we often get into is when we try to fulfill our needs by turning to something other than God to fill our voids. Friend, it is only when we look to Christ to satisfy the deepest needs of our lives that we will find true fulfillment. Don't buy into the lie that there are self-made men and women. Those whose lives are truly blessed have turned to God for their needs to be fulfilled and have started a divine partnership with him.

THE TAKEAWAY: There is no such thing as a self-made man but there is such a thing as a self-destroyed man. Don't destroy the plans God has for you by ignoring God.

MARCH 6TH

Acts 23:11—"The following night the Lord stood near Paul and said, "Take courage!"

God wants you to have courage. Courage to stand up to your greatest fears, to try something different, to go against the negative flow you see at work or around others. Courage to dream big and be who God wants you to be, to go back to school or apply for that job. Friend, do you know why we can and should have courage? The answer is in today's verse, "The Lord stood near Paul." We should have courage because God is standing with us.

THE TAKEAWAY: You can pray about courage, but God won't move your feet. At some point, you have to step out in faith.

MARCH 7TH

Hebrews 4:12—"For the word of God is alive and active."

It's not over until God says it's over! It doesn't matter what has happened in your finances, marriage, family, or job. It isn't over until God says it is over. If you stand on God's Word you are standing on an unmovable foundation. As you go through your day, just remember, if you want the abundant life, you have to have the obedient life. Obey God's Word and see what God will do.

THE TAKEAWAY: Don't put a period where God has a comma. You might think that something in your life is finished. Just because there is a waiting period or trials doesn't mean that God is through with that area of your life.

MARCH 8TH

Isaiah 43:19—"See, I am doing a new thing!"

God wants to do something new in your life. God wants to do something new in your marriage. God wants to do something new in your destiny. However, sometimes we don't like change. Sometimes we don't like to try something we aren't comfortable with doing. Ultimately God wants to bless you, but that avenue of blessing often comes when we do or try something new. As you go through this day, don't be afraid to pursue God in areas you never have before.

THE TAKEAWAY: *New* can be a scary word. Don't let new scare you. Let new excite you.

MARCH 9TH

Psalm 25:4-5—"Show me your ways, Lord, teach me your paths. Guide me in your truth and teach me, for you are God my savior, and my hope is in you all day long."

Do you want to be blessed? Pray this above prayer often. I want to encourage you today, wherever you are, take a moment to silently pray this verse or say it out loud. You might even write this verse down on a note card and post it or carry it with you. There is power in prayer and asking God to show you his ways.

THE TAKEAWAY: Praying might not change our circumstance, but it will change us. Pray.

MARCH 10TH

Psalm 144:15—"Blessed is the people whose God is the Lord."

Nobody is a true atheist! Everyone serves and believes in some type of god. For some people, money, fame, or power are their gods. People have served numerous things. However, our Heavenly Father is the Lord. He is Lord over all! If you want a life that is fulfilled and truly blessed, focus your life on serving the Lord.

THE TAKEAWAY: Truth is not based on feelings. Truth is based on fact. Put your trust in God regardless of how you feel or what you see before you.

MARCH 11TH

Psalm 146:7—"The Lord sets prisoners free."

Come out of that prison! You might not be behind bars, but you might be locked up behind guilt, worry, fear, regret, loneliness, sin, anger, bitterness, or anxiety. God wants you out of prison! Jesus Christ died on the cross and rose from the grave so we could have freedom.

THE TAKEAWAY: The doors to your prison are open. What prison cell do you need to come out of today?

MARCH 12TH

Romans 12:21—"Do not be overcome by evil, but overcome evil with good."

Right now, you might have someone in your life who is difficult and causing you a lot of grief. Maybe it's a coworker, family member, or acquaintance. Friend, if someone is trying to hurt your life, don't fight fire with fire because the only thing that happens is both people get burnt. The way to fight against whomever is bringing pain into your life is by showing them unconditional grace and God's love. Overcome evil with good!

THE TAKEAWAY: Identify the people in your life who cause you the most problems, and start attacking them with the weapons of love, grace, and mercy.

MARCH 13TH

Acts 26:28—"Do you think that in such a short time you can persuade me to be a Christian?"

King Agrippa tells the Apostle Paul, "Do you think that in such a short time you can persuade me?" Friend, don't live an "almost" type of life. If you almost finish the race that means you didn't. If you almost live, that means you died. If you almost succeed, that means you failed. God didn't intend for you to almost have an abundant life; he wants you to actually have an abundant life.

THE TAKEAWAY: Where in your walk with God are you almost there? Go over the line!

MARCH 14TH

Psalm 46:1-2—"God is our refuge and strength, an ever-present help in trouble. Therefore we will not fear, though the earth give way."

If you trust God, everything will be OK. As soon as you read that, you might have thought, "You don't know what I am going through." If you have a lot weighing you down today and are feeling overwhelmed, ask God to help you see your problem from his point of view instead of your own. If you start to observe your problems through God's vantage point, he will help your perspective change. When you give your burdens to God, remember that everything will be OK.

THE TAKEAWAY: Many times, giving our burdens to God is easier said than done. If you give your burdens to God and they find their way back to you, keep giving them to God until they don't come back.

MARCH 15TH

Ecclesiastes 7:12—"Wisdom is a shelter."

If you want to protect your life and live a life of abundance, you have to use wisdom in all your choices. Jim Rohn says, "Discipline is the bridge between goals and accomplishment." One of the wisest things we can do is make ourselves more disciplined. Just think how becoming more disciplined in what you eat, how you spend your money, and what you allow yourself to think about would bless your life. This isn't popular, but when you are wise and disciplined, you can't help but be blessed!

THE TAKEAWAY: You will either be disciplined in your life or not. The key to becoming disciplined is submitting your will to God.

MARCH 16TH

Psalm 118:24—"The Lord has done it this very day; let us rejoice today and be glad."

Today isn't your day, it's God's day. He is the one who made it, and he desires you to win in life. If today is God's day, guess who has ownership of the problems you might face today? God! The only issue is that sometimes we try to keep the problems that, in all reality, should be given to God. I want to encourage you to give God your day and all the worries that might go along with it!

THE TAKEAWAY: God wants you to cast your cares on him. Refuse to take back problems that God wants you to lay at his feet.

MARCH 17TH

Psalm 48:14—"God is our God forever and ever; he will be our guide even to the end."

Have you ever been lost? I don't mean missing an exit, but I mean completely lost? Nothing is more discouraging and frustrating. Sometimes in our lives we get lost in what to do in our family, finances, and relationships. Friend, God promises to be our guide throughout life. However, a guide can only help us if we are listening. If you need guidance, take a moment today to ask God to guide you and then listen!

THE TAKEAWAY: It is very difficult to listen to two different voices at the same time. What noise or voice in your life do you need to turn down so you can hear God's voice better?

MARCH 18TH

John 8:44—"When the devil lies, he speaks his native language, for he is a liar and the father of lies."

If you're alive, the devil is trying to lie to you today. He wants to tell you that you can't succeed. He wants to tell you that you can't be healed. He wants to tell you that your situation can't be changed. When we buy into the devil's lies, we always assume the worst. My former pastor said, "Believe the best until you are sure of the worst." God has greatness in store for you; don't believe the devil's lies.

THE TAKEAWAY: Remember the first step to any type of bondage is to believe a lie.

MARCH 19TH

Proverbs 11:30—"The fruit of the righteous is a tree of life."

We are all leaving a trail behind us. What type of trail are you leaving? Are you leaving a trail of goodness/love/mercy/encouragement, or are you leaving a trail of selfishness/anger/bitterness/unforgiveness? I want to encourage you today: you are leaving a mark on this world with your life, so make sure to leave a positive legacy.

THE TAKEAWAY: There are only three things you can do with your life. You can spend it, waste it, or invest it. Which one are you doing?

MARCH 20TH

Proverbs 15:10—"The one who hates correction will die."
Proverbs 15:31—"Whoever heeds life-giving correction will be at home among the wise."

None of us enjoy being criticized or corrected. Correction might seem painful, but it can be beneficial. When somebody who loves you corrects you, don't write off what they say, consider it. When somebody who doesn't love you corrects you, chances are that much of what they said you need to forget, but even then, you can learn from them. None of us are perfect, and we all need to be open to correction.

THE TAKEAWAY: To do great things for God, you must be teachable. A lack of heeding correction has kept many good leaders from becoming great leaders.

MARCH 21ST

Proverbs 12:16—"The prudent overlook an insult."

"Life is or should be fair" is not a statement you will find in the Bible. At some point in time, all of us will get insulted or mistreated by others. But not all of us overlook the insult or hurt. Some people are easily offended, and I guarantee those people live a miserable life. The only way not to get hurt by people is to live a life of a hermit. Don't forget that others have overlooked your insults and hurts to them so you should do the same.

THE TAKEAWAY: Don't be a hurt hoarder.

MARCH 22ND

Romans 8:31—"If God is for us, who can be against us?"

Have you ever felt like everyone was against you? Sometimes in life we might feel like even those we love have it in for us. I have good news for you, God does not have it in for you and he is in your corner. God is for you even when you make mistakes. He might not be supporting your actions, but he sure loves and supports you. "If God is for us who can be against us?"

THE TAKEAWAY: God is in the grand stands of life cheering you on. Just know today God is with you.

MARCH 23ND

Proverbs 21:30—"There is no wisdom, no insight, no plan, that can succeed against the Lord."

When your life is not submitted to God, there is no bunker, bankroll, or barricade that can protect you. However, when your life is submitted to God, there is no way you can fail. You might have setbacks, but when every area of your life is given over to God, you are able to walk in the power and strength of God. If you are struggling to give an area of your life over to God, surrender it to him today.

THE TAKEAWAY: God has never been defeated. You can know that without any doubt, when you partner with him, great and amazing things will be in your future.

MARCH 24TH

Philippians 3:13—"But one thing I do: Forgetting what is behind and straining toward what is ahead."

Let go of whatever is haunting you from your past! We all make mistakes, and we all get hurt by others. Regardless if you have hurt someone in your life or someone has hurt you, you have to let it go. Michael Jordon once said, "I missed over 9000 shots in my career, I've lost over 300 games...I've failed over and over in my life. And that is why I succeed." Don't let pain that occurred in the past bring pain to your future.

THE TAKEAWAY: Stop looking back. When you are looking to the past, there is no way you can run to the future!

MARCH 25TH

Romans 8:35—*"Who shall separate us from the love of Christ?"*

Good is faithful. In the good times and bad times, God is faithful. When we are up or down, God is faithful. No matter what the circumstance or situation, God is faithful. Read the lyrics of this old hymn:

> *Great is thy faithfulness, O God my Father;*
> *There is no shadow of turning with Thee;*
> *Thou changest not, Thy compassion's, they fail not;*
> *As Thou hast been, Thou forever will be.*

God is faithful even though we aren't perfect!

THE TAKEAWAY: We need to trust the power of God, but we also must trust the plan of God. If you think God is taking your life on a detour, just know he has the final destination in mind.

MARCH 26TH

Psalm 102:5—"In my distress I groan aloud."

Sometimes, I can be the king of groaning. I can complain with the best of them. However, I am challenged to turn my loud groaning into loud praising of God. I am challenged to turn my loud groaning into thankfulness for the blessings God has given me. I want to challenge you today to turn your groaning volume on low and your praising and thankfulness volume on high.

THE TAKEAWAY: When you grumble and complain, you become weaker. Conversely, when you are thankful, you become stronger.

MARCH 27TH

Galatians 5:1—"It was for freedom that Christ has set us free."

When I see police lights behind me, I naturally pull over. However, if an average Joe attempted to pull me over, I would probably just keep driving. Why? Because, police have the authority to pull me over and issue me a ticket. The average Joe does not have that authority. Maybe the devil has tried to tell you that your past mistakes can't be forgiven, or that you can't be healed, or that you will always struggle with an addiction. However, that is not what God says, and ultimately, he is the only one who has all authority. God declares that you are free; so don't listen to the devil. Listen to God!

THE TAKEAWAY: Is there an area of your life that you need to take back from the enemy? God says you're free, so that settles it.

MARCH 28TH

Luke 1:37—"For no word from God will ever fail."

Don't quit! Today you might be tempted to quit on a job, quit on a spouse, quit on a dream, quit on yourself, or even quit on God. Wherever you're tempted to quit, don't do it! Remember, nothing is impossible with God! Let this quote from Josh Billings inspire you, "Consider the postage stamp: its usefulness consists in the ability to stick to one thing till it gets there." Bottom line…Don't quit!

THE TAKEAWAY: The difference between winners and losers is the point at which they are willing to quit.

MARCH 29TH

Romans 3:23—"For all have sinned."

Stop judging people! Every person struggles with hurts, hang-ups, and habits. Not only do we hurt others when we judge them, but we also hurt ourselves. Once we start judging others, we deceive ourselves into thinking we are better than that person we are judging. Friend, focus on overcoming your own shortcomings and then spend time praying, instead of judging, others to overcome theirs.

THE TAKEAWAY: You can't keep your eyes on Jesus and focus on someone else's problems at the same time. Keep your eyes on Jesus.

MARCH 30TH

Psalm 85:12—"The Lord will indeed give what is good."

When we give into worry, it is a sign we are not trusting God. Basically, worry is the opposite of faith and the two don't coincide with each other. We can learn a great deal from a quote by Erma Bombeck, "Worry is like a rocking chair: it gives you something to do but never gets you anywhere." If you are tempted to worry, start starving worry and feeding your faith and trust in God.

THE TAKEAWAY: At times, we have to make ourselves trust what we know, not what we see.

MARCH 31ST

James 1:19—"Everyone should be quick to listen, slow to speak and slow to become angry."

Will Rogers once said, "People who fly into a rage always make a bad landing." When we give into our anger we not only harm others, but we hurt ourselves. If you're struggling with anger, put these three basic principles into action today:

1) Be quick to listen.
2) Be slow to speak.
3) Be slow to anger.

THE TAKEAWAY: If we give into anger, it will cost us more than we are willing to pay.

APRIL 1ST

Acts 11:9—"Do not call anything impure that God has made clean."

A guilty conscience stinks! All of us have dealt with guilt more than once in our lifetime. However, the good news is that when we admit our mistakes and sins to God, he forgives us and makes us clean. You heard me correctly, clean. In fact, the verse today says, "Do not call impure what God has made clean." Friend, if you're feeling guilty, take your mistakes and guilty conscience to God. If he is the one who cleanses you, you are clean.

THE TAKEAWAY: Only the sacrifice of Jesus can pay for our sins. When you sin, just remember Jesus paid for all of your sins and mine.

APRIL 2ND

Psalm 27:14—"Wait for the Lord; be strong and take heart and wait for the Lord."

Waiting on God takes courage! It is easy to just settle for second best. It is easy to agree to just good enough. But God doesn't want you to have a marriage that is just good enough. God doesn't want you to have a job that is just good enough. God doesn't want you to have a life that is just good enough. God wants you to have a more than enough life. But to have that full life you must be patient and wait for God's best.

THE TAKEAWAY: Are you struggling to wait on God? I promise if you wait on God, the wait will be well worth it!

APRIL 3RD

Deuteronomy 15:6—"For the Lord your God will bless you as he has promised, and you will lend to many nations but you will borrow from none. You will rule over many nations but none will rule over you."

God wants your life to be full of his favor. If you have a 12-ounce can and 8 ounces is full of dirt, you only have 4 ounces left for water. If you want 12 full ounces of water, you have to throw out the dirt. God wants to fill our lives full with his favor, but if we have allowed the dirt of this life to fill us, there is precious little room for God's favor. Today, empty yourself of the dirt of this life, and let God fill your life with his blessings!

THE TAKEAWAY: We have to make room for God's blessings in our lives. What needs to be removed from your life so you can be blessed?

APRIL 4TH

1 Corinthians 1:31—"Therefore, as it is written: "Let the one who boasts boast in the Lord.""

At times, we can be good at telling people how terrible things are in our lives. Sometimes we can even excel at sharing our trials with others. But friend, that isn't what God wants. God wants us to boast about him, not the issues we all face. Instead of telling God how big your problems are, start telling your problems how big your God is. Boast in the Lord and be blessed!

THE TAKEAWAY: There is power in our words. Use your words to bless and not curse.

APRIL 5TH

Joshua 6:20—"The wall collapsed."

Do you need a breakthrough from God for your life? Joshua marched the people of God around the city of Jericho and the wall collapsed. Friend, God can also make the walls come down in any area of your life. In fact, you might be just one day or one hour away from a major breakthrough. The key is doing what God tells you to do. God told his people to march around Jericho seven times. God might be telling you to love those who hurt you, forgive those who harm you, or care for those who despise you. Do what God tells you to do and you will have that breakthrough.

THE TAKEAWAY: Is there a wall in your life that needs to come down? Obey God even if what he asks of you seems crazy. He always has a plan.

APRIL 6TH

Psalm 133:3—"The Lord bestows his blessing."

God is a heavenly Father who wants to bless his children. However, if you want to be blessed, you have to be bold! Throughout the Bible, when people were bold in their prayers, bold in their actions, and bold in their requests, God poured out his blessings. Every single day we have the opportunity to talk to the most powerful person in the universe, God. He can handle all of our bold and big requests.

THE TAKEAWAY: There is a spiritual principle at work in our prayers. You can't ask small and receive big. If you ask small, you receive small. So, ask big!

APRIL 7TH

Genesis 39:12—"She caught him by his cloak and said, 'Come to bed with me!' But he left his cloak in her hand and ran out of the house."

None of us are perfect and we have all sinned. But the best way to avoid sinning is to run from temptation. You don't have to go to Bible College to learn how to run. You don't have to memorize the Bible to learn how to run. You don't even have to join a Bible study to learn how to run. Whenever you're tempted to sin, run from it! Joseph avoided sexual sin because he ran.

THE TAKEAWAY: What temptation are you running to that you should be running away from?

APRIL 8TH

Jeremiah 1:5—"Before I formed you in the womb I knew you."

Have you ever met someone who doesn't believe in miracles? Or, maybe that someone is you. Do you know why you should believe in miracles? Because you are one! God formed you in your mother's womb, and God only creates masterpieces. There are many things that had to go perfectly for you to be born. God's plans for your life are so much larger than you can comprehend.

THE TAKEAWAY: Have you ever compared yourself to someone else? If you have, stop! Nothing good comes from comparing ourselves to others. God created you, and he made you exactly how he planned.

APRIL 9TH

Matthew 18:19—"Again, I tell you that if two of you on earth agree about anything they ask for, it will be done for them by my Father in heaven."

Who are you agreeing with…God or the devil? The devil will constantly try to put you down, bring up your past, or convince you that you are a failure. Are you agreeing with him or with God? It is easy to believe the junk the devil tries to throw at us. On the other hand, God says you are more than a conqueror. Today, make sure you are agreeing with God and what he has to say about you and not the devil.

THE TAKEAWAY: There is so much power in agreement. What agreements, perhaps even accidentally, have you made with the enemy that you need to stop making?

APRIL 10TH

Psalm 128:1—"Blessed are all who fear the Lord, who walk in obedience to him."

Are you struggling today? Are you a little tight? It is possible that you could be facing issues because you are walking in your own ways? It happens to me all the time because it is so natural for me want to do things my own way. The problem with this notion is my way will always fail. If you want to succeed, walk in obedience to God.

THE TAKEAWAY: Oftentimes, doing things God's way can be uncomfortable. However, many things that are good for us are uncomfortable as well.

APRIL 11TH

Zephaniah 3:20—"When I restore your fortunes before your very eyes."

One of the most powerful things God does is restore the things in our lives that have been lost or stolen by sin, other people's sin, or our bad choices. Friend, God wants to restore to you what you feel like has been stolen. Maybe it is innocence, money, an opportunity, or you name it. God is so powerful he can restore what we once had and even more. Hang in there.

THE TAKEAWAY: What has been lost or stolen from you that you want God to restore? Don't worry about what you have lost. Focus on God and his ability to turn things around for you.

APRIL 12TH

Psalm 71:14—"As for me, I will always have hope."

No matter what is happening in our country, around the world or in your life, God wants you to have hope. Notice we don't acquire hope just once. We can continuously have hope. God is for you and not against you. Don't let go of hope over your life, career, health, finances, relationships, you name it.

THE TAKEAWAY: Expectancy is the breeding ground for miracles. Get your hopes up!

APRIL 13TH

Psalm 68:19—"Praise be to the Lord, to God our Savior, who daily bears our burdens."

Are you doing some heavy lifting today? I'm not talking about lifting weights or suitcases. I am talking about lifting your cares, concerns, hurts, and mistakes. Those loads can be really heavy! Friend, God doesn't just want to carry our burdens; he wants to daily bear our burdens. So, if you're getting a little worn out today, let God do the heavy lifting for you!

THE TAKEAWAY: You can carry your burdens or God can carry them for you. We have to make a choice each day who will do the lifting.

APRIL 14TH

Mark 9:35—"Anyone who wants to be first must be the very last, and the servant to all."

How do you succeed in life? How do you become a true success? Millions of people have asked this question. Jesus answers this question very simply. You succeed in life by putting other people first. We may not fully understand this concept, but when we put others needs first, our needs get met. When we bring hope and healing to others, our lives experience hope and healing. If you want to live a life that counts, remember to put others first.

THE TAKEAWAY: There is never a man emptier than one who is full of himself. How can you put others who are in your life ahead of yourself?

APRIL 15TH

2 Corinthians 4:8—"We are hard pressed on every side."

This scripture really hits home sometimes. Today, you might be feeling hard pressed on every side. Most of us don't like feeling that kind of pressure in life, but after we go through a time of pressing, we come out stronger. When a clay pot is put in a kiln, it either cracks or solidifies and becomes stronger. When we rely strictly on our own strength, we will crack every time. But when we rely on God, the pressures we face solidify us and make us resilient.

THE TAKEAWAY: If you're going through some pressure today, just know God is using that pressure to make you stronger.

APRIL 16TH

Psalm 83:12—"Let us take possession."

Today could be a day of destiny for you. Are you just drifting through life, or have you made a strategic choice to take possession of God's blessing and destiny for your life? It is important to pray, fast, and study God's Word. But there comes a point in our lives when we have to make a choice: Will we simply just exist, or will we thrive? Friend, God wants you to take possession of your destiny. Step out today, and trust God where you haven't trusted him before.

THE TAKEAWAY: There is a big difference between surviving and thriving. What changes do you need to make to thrive?

APRIL 17TH

Genesis 1:27—"God created mankind in his own image."

You were created to succeed. Yes, that's right! You might say, "How do you know that?" Friend, name me one time in the Bible where God failed. Good luck finding that! God created you in his own image. He wants you to flourish in life. Let me leave you with a quote from Jeremy Collier: "Everyone has a fair turn to be as great as he pleases." You are created in God's image.

THE TAKEAWAY: Greatness and significance are choices. What choice do you make today?

APRIL 18TH

Mark 8:8—"The people ate and were satisfied."

This verse comes from the story of Jesus feeding the four thousand. I am not sure what miracle was greater: the fact that Jesus fed four thousand people, or the fact that those who ate were satisfied. Oftentimes, when we try to find satisfaction in people, money, substances, or titles, we tend to feel empty and wanting. Our lives will only become fulfilled when we look to Jesus for satisfaction and significance. The only way to be fully satisfied in this life is to turn daily to Jesus as our source for wisdom, grace, and love.

THE TAKEAWAY: Where have you turned for fulfillment? Whatever you yield to, you will be full of.

APRIL 19TH

2 Corinthians 1:3-4—"Praise be to the God and Father of our Lord Jesus Christ, the Father of compassion and the God of all comfort, who comforts us in all our troubles."

Life can be rough! Life can be painful and sometimes difficult to understand, but God gives us a promise. He does not promise to remove the hurtful things in our lives, but he promises to comfort us and to help us get through the painful times of life. Friend, if you need God's comfort in your life today, hand over the pain and those hurts you have been struggling with. If you pick them back up, hand them back to God. God wants to comfort you.

THE TAKEAWAY: Comfort and trust go hand in hand. There is power when we worship God, especially during the painful times.

APRIL 20TH

Psalm 92:15—"The Lord is upright; he is my Rock, and there is no wickedness in him."

Have you ever experienced someone being nice to you, but it wasn't genuine? They were simply being nice to you to get something from you. Friend, this is the exact opposite of the purpose God has for desiring to know you. God wants to know you in a real and powerful way, not so he can get something from you, but so he can give into your life. There is no wickedness in him. God loves you and wants to give you his favor so you can be blessed and so you can bless others.

THE TAKEAWAY: Have you tried to use people to get something from them? God doesn't want us to use people. He wants us to freely give to people.

APRIL 21ST

Acts 5:39—"You will only find yourselves fighting against God."

There is a constant battle that we all have to face each day in our lives. Either we are going to do things our way or God's way. Friend, what areas in your life are you tempted to do things your way? Let me tell you from experience, it is always more painful to do things our own way. Allow God to have complete control of your life when you might be tempted to do things your way instead of his. When we fight God, we always lose. But when we let him lead our lives, we always win.

THE TAKEAWAY: Have you heard the term *control freak*? Sometimes, we can struggle with attempting to have complete control over our lives. There is so much blessing when we truly give things over God.

APRIL 22ND

Psalm 55:22—"Cast your cares on the Lord and he will sustain you."

I am thankful we don't have to carry all our troubles, trials, and burdens. We can give those to God. Let me give you five reasons why we shouldn't worry:

1) Worry doesn't accomplish anything (Mathew 6:27—"Can any one of you by worrying add a single hour to your life?").
2) Worry hurts us (Proverbs 12:25—"Anxiety weighs down the heart.").
3) Worry is the opposite of trusting God (Philippians 4:6—"Do not be anxious about anything, but in every situation, by prayer and petition, with thanksgiving, present your requests to God.").
4) Worry puts your focus in the wrong direction (Proverbs 3:5—"Trust in the Lord with all your heart.").
5) Worry isn't the will of God (John 14:27—"Peace I leave with you; my peace I give you.").

THE TAKEAWAY: Why worry?

APRIL 23RD

Psalm 147:3—"He heals the brokenhearted and binds up their wounds."

A few years ago, my wife woke up in serious pain. She went to the doctor and he said she needed an outpatient surgery. She had surgery and is pain free today, Praise God! However, notice that the doctor had to hurt her in order to heal her. The surgery had temporary pain and so did the recovery, but she is pain free today. Oftentimes, when God brings healing to our lives, there might be some hurt in the process in order to bring the healing. God desires for your family, relationships, and peace of mind to be healed. Don't give up if there is a little hurt along the way.

THE TAKEAWAY: Would you ponder this thought today? Sometimes doing the right thing is going to hurt.

APRIL 24TH

2 Corinthians 5:17—"Therefore, if anyone is in Christ, the new creation has come: The old has gone, the new is here!"

Is there an area of your life where you need a new beginning? If so, I have good news for you. God specializes in giving people brand-new starts! God desires to free you from your present entanglements so you can enjoy future blessings. Don't let the devil make your life more complicated. You can get a new start today. The devil will try to tempt you into believing you can't get a new beginning in some area of your life. Don't listen to him; he is lying!

THE TAKEAWAY: God does want you to have a fresh start. However, the key to the fresh start is it comes from being in Christ.

APRIL 25TH

Mark 9:23—"Everything is possible for one who believes."

A couple was celebrating their sixty-five years of marriage and was asked how they stayed together for so long. The wife replied, "We were born in a time where if something was broken you fixed it; you didn't throw it away." In our world today, people are quick to throw away dreams, relationships, jobs, and opportunities just because times get tough. Friend, if you're struggling in an area today, don't give up. God can fix anything!

THE TAKEAWAY: One key to God fixing our broken lives is to start by simply believing he can.

APRIL 26TH

Psalm 62:11-12—"One thing God has spoken, two things have I heard: Power belongs to you, God, and with you, Lord, is unfailing love."

If you are facing a big problem, God is bigger.
If you are dealing with a strong hurt, God is stronger.
If you are encountering mighty opposition, God is mightier.
If you are neck-deep in confusion, God's wisdom is deeper.

Friend, no matter where you are at today, God is all-powerful. Invite him into your pain or whatever you are struggling with, and you will see things begin to change.

THE TAKEAWAY: Oftentimes, we invite Jesus into our hearts, which is a great thing! However, have you considered inviting him into your pain?

APRIL 27TH

Joshua 1:5—"I will never leave you nor forsake you."

When you don't know what to do, God is there. When your heart is broken, God is there. When you mess up and it's embarrassing, God is there. When you overcome a trial, God is there. When you achieve a great victory, God is there. Friend, God won't leave you, no matter where your life takes you.

THE TAKEAWAY: Don't ever let the devil tell you that God isn't there. He is a good God and he is not leaving your side!

APRIL 28TH

1 Corinthians 10:13—"No temptation has overtaken you."

Have you ever felt trapped? I have! But, whenever we go through life and feel trapped, that is a lie. In today's verse, God promises that, "No temptation has overtaken you." That means no addiction is too strong, no mistake is too wrong, no failure is too great where almighty God cannot turn it around. So, if you feel trapped today by fear, anxiety, or anything else, God wants you to know there is always a way out. God has the power to take us from pain to victory.

THE TAKEAWAY: There is no prison cell that can contain the love and power of God.

APRIL 29TH

Proverbs 17:28—"Even fools are thought wise if they keep silent."

You can't unsay words. Once they have been said, their power to heal or hurt has been released. Oftentimes, we operate under the principle of, "Don't just stand there, do something." However, it might be wiser when we encounter the stresses of life for our response to be, "Don't just do something, stand there." When life gets rocky with family and friends, sometimes the best things we say are the things we don't.

THE TAKEAWAY: Where in your life do you need to gain control of your tongue and words?

APRIL 30TH

1 Samuel 17:48—"David ran quickly toward the battle line to meet him."

How are you handling your Goliath? We all have a Goliath of some kind in our lives. Our Goliath might not be a Philistine giant, but it might be a health problem, stress, worry, or some type of relationship issue. Most people run from their problems. Notice David ran toward his. Friend if you run to God with your problem, you can then run to your problem to conquer it. Put your running shoes on today and slay the Goliath in your life.

THE TAKEAWAY: What are you running from? Run to God and get his power to slay the giant.

MAY 1ST

1 Peter 5:7—"Cast all your anxiety on him because he cares for you."

Recently, my wife and I had a whirlwind week as we sold our home and purchased another one. Through that crazy week and into today, I realized that often we do the opposite of this verse. Many times, we embrace our anxiety instead of casting it to God. Giving God your worries is not about never worrying, but it is about trusting God, worshiping God, loving God, and refocusing your life on him when life gets crazy. God wants us to embrace him, not our worries, and he will take care of our anxieties.

THE TAKEAWAY: What real tangible ways can you start embracing God and not your problems?

MAY 2ND

Psalm 3:8—"From the Lord comes deliverance."

Oftentimes, we act as if the scripture reads, "From the banker comes deliverance." Or, "From the government comes deliverance." Or maybe, "From the doctor comes deliverance." However, we will never have true contentment and blessing in our lives until we make God the source of our very being. God loves you today, and when we turn to him, he releases real power into our lives.

THE TAKEAWAY: When we are in a trial, the devil wants our eyes focused on the problem. Take your eyes off the problem and put them on the answer, Jesus.

MAY 3RD

Psalm 89:47—"Remember how fleeting is my life."

Don't wait until tomorrow to tell those you love that you love them.
Don't wait until tomorrow to forgive those who hurt you.
Don't wait until tomorrow to take responsibility for your mistakes.
Don't wait until tomorrow to receive God's forgiveness and grace for your mistakes.
Don't wait until tomorrow to try what you have always wanted to try.
Don't wait until tomorrow to live life on the offensive.
Don't wait until tomorrow to believe God for something that seems impossible in your life.

THE TAKEAWAY: What have you dreamed about doing that you haven't begun? Start today.

MAY 4TH

Isaiah 55:9—"As the heavens are higher than the earth, so are my ways higher than your ways and my thoughts than your thoughts."

God is too...

Mysterious for me to define
Obvious for me to deny
Great for me to manage
Loving for me to mistrust
Mighty for me to dismiss
Powerful for me to battle
Kind for me to ignore
Right for me to go wrong

Trust God with what you are going through today. He loves you!

THE TAKEAWAY: If you're attempting to put God in a box, it won't happen. If you are striving to fully understand God, it won't happen in this lifetime. He is too big and too loving to fully comprehend.

MAY 5TH

1 Corinthians 15:57—"But thanks be to God! He gives us the victory through our Lord Jesus Christ."

The number of home runs Babe Ruth had when he retired was 714. He was the king of home runs. The amount of strikeouts Babe Ruth had when he retired was 1330. He was also the king of strikeouts. Even though he had 1330 strikeouts, numerous baseball historians to this day consider him the greatest baseball player ever. Friend, just because you have had some strikeouts in life doesn't mean you aren't a champion. Don't quit and don't give up!

THE TAKEAWAY: Have you had a strikeout in life recently? If so, don't stay in the dugout. Get back up to the plate and start swinging again.

MAY 6TH

Jeremiah 1:5—"Before I formed you in the womb I knew you."

God can't bless who you want to be. He can only bless who he created you to be. Friend, God knew you before you were born. He had plans for you before you took your first breath. Don't try to act like someone else. You are a masterpiece created by God. Don't strive to imitate someone. Be who God has called you to be!

THE TAKEAWAY: If there is something about you that you don't love, please consider this truth - God loves ALL of you!

MAY 7TH

Luke 6:28—"Bless those who curse you."

What do you do when people mistreat you? How do you handle a situation when someone is mean to you? Martin Luther King Jr. once said, "Darkness cannot drive out darkness," which means if someone mistreats you, causing that person harm in return won't solve the issue. The answer to resolving the painful issues of life is simple, "Bless those who curse you." If you fight fire with fire, the only thing that happens is both parties get burnt.

THE TAKEAWAY: Do you have someone in your life who you are in conflict with? If so, don't fight fire with fire. Fight fire with blessings!

MAY 8TH

Colossians 1:16—"For in him all things were created: things in heaven and on earth, visible and invisible, whether thrones or powers or rulers or authorities; all things have been created through him and for him."

Today, what is going on in your life that needs to be changed? Is it an issue that you think is just too big for God to change? Friend, this verse says, "In him all things were created." If God created all things, he can create a solution to whatever problem you are facing. Know that God deeply loves you, and he has the answer for what has been attacking your life.

THE TAKEAWAY: The greatest limit on your life is you.

MAY 9TH

Psalm 90:12—"Teach us to number our days."

Oftentimes, we are consumed with numbers! How much do I weigh, what is my salary, how high is my cholesterol, and what is my credit score? The one number we don't focus on too much is how long we will live. Friend, God has a set number of days for each of us. There is a country song by Tim McGraw that goes, "Live like you were dying." Don't play life safe! Be bold, take risks, love freely, and partner with God to make every day he gives you count.

THE TAKEAWAY: Where are you playing it safe in your life? Is it time to step out in faith?

MAY 10TH

Joshua 24:15—"Then choose for yourselves this day whom you will serve."

You have the freedom to make choices, but you do not get freedom from the results of those choices. Successful people most often make healthy choices. Many times people dealing with the pain of life have made unhealthy choices. Today, make the decision to start making small healthy choices. Healthy choices typically are more difficult to make but they are worth it.

THE TAKEAWAY: Most often our success is determined by our choices. Typically, the easy choices can hurt us while the harder choices end up being the ones that help us. Is there a hard choice you need to make today?

MAY 11TH

Proverbs 29:18—"Where there is no revelation, people cast off restraint."

God wants you to be a leader! Two keys to having vision for your life are:

1) You have to see the invisible. Leaders don't see situations as they are; they see situations as they can become.
2) You have to hear the inaudible. Leaders purposely turn off the busyness of life so they can hear God's voice.

God loves you, and he wants you to be a leader!

THE TAKEAWAY: What can you do to see and hear God more clearly?

MAY 12TH

Matthew 5:45—"He causes his sun to rise on the evil and the good, and sends rain on the righteous and the unrighteous."

No matter who you are, there will be times when you are going to face setbacks. Regardless of your last name or place in life, if you are rich or poor, you will face obstacles. But friend, God wants you to change how you view the adversities that appear in your life because your setback is a set up for a comeback. God allows trials to occur, but we can control how we will respond in those trials.

THE TAKEAWAY: Do you view problems as problems? Or do you view problems as opportunities?

MAY 13TH

Psalm 30:5—"For his anger lasts only a moment, but his favor lasts a lifetime."

Today, we are going to look at something very unpopular: the anger of God. God is our Father and as we know at times, children do things to anger their fathers. In fact, when a good father is angry with his child, it is because his child is doing something that is destructive to himself or herself. Friend, do you know God never gets angry with us because of who we are? He gets angry because sometimes we are disobedient and make unhealthy choices that will bring harm to our lives. However, God wants you to have his favor at work, in your relationships, in your thought life, in dealings with your money, in everything your hand touches, God wants you to have his favor. Healthy choices go hand in hand with God's favor.

THE TAKEAWAY: Are you making healthy or hurtful choices today?

MAY 14TH

Psalm 22:5—"To you they cried out and were saved; in you they trusted and were not put to shame."

What a miracle of God! Not only does God promise to save but also he promises not to disappoint. One of the reasons God can promise not to disappoint is because he is the only one who truly knows what we need. Many times, the reality is we don't even know what we need. If you will keep following God, you can count on the fact that you won't be disappointed.

THE TAKEAWAY: Some of the most gracious acts of God were the times he didn't answer our prayers the way we wanted. Think about that statement and reflect on those unanswered prayers in your life.

MAY 15TH

Psalm 28:8—"The Lord is the strength of his people."

As we start another day, where will you draw strength? The Lord is the strength of his people. Many Christians try to get their strength from friends, advice, their own will power, or even the church. Even though these things can be good, we must ultimately find our strength in God alone. Whatever happens this week, make sure you are looking to God for strength. Make sure you are not leaning solely on your own knowledge, skill, or understanding. God desires that we would win and overcome in life, but that only happens when he is our strength. As you face this day, just remember where your true strength comes from.

THE TAKEAWAY: Our power is only as strong as our source.

MAY 16TH

2 Corinthians 1:3-4—"Praise be to the God and Father of our Lord Jesus Christ, the Father of compassion and the God of all comfort, who comforts us in all our troubles, so that we can comfort those in any trouble with the comfort we ourselves receive from God."

If you need comfort in your life today, God can comfort you. Regardless of what the situation is, when it happened, or how bad it might be, thank God he comforts us in every area! However, the Bible teaches after we have been comforted to let God use us to comfort others. When we use our troubled times to comfort others, we are allowing what brought us pain to bring healing to others.

THE TAKEAWAY: God never wastes a hurt. Think about how God can use your pain to heal others.

MAY 17TH

1 Corinthians 16:13—"Be on your guard; stand firm in the faith; be courageous; be strong."

Courage! It isn't a topic we normally hear about in a sermon or something we typically read about in books. But it is one of the keys to having the life you have always dreamed of having. In fact, all great men and women have been people of courage. It takes courage to truly live life, but it doesn't take courage to simply exist. Do you need courage to apply for that job, to start school, to leave a relationship, to start a relationship, to tell a friend about God's love, to try something new, to say no when everyone is saying yes, to change an action, or to believe God for something better in your life? Whatever it is, I want you to know you can be a person of courage. It takes courage to live a life with no regrets and excellence.

THE TAKEAWAY: Courage doesn't mean the absence of fear. It means action in the face of fear.

MAY 18TH

2 Corinthians 5:17—"Therefore, if anyone is in Christ, the new creation has come: The old has gone, the new is here!"

Are you in Christ or into yourself? Often, the most painful times of my life were caused because I was overly focused on me. And the other side is true as well. Many times, the best and most blessed times of my life occurred when I was truly living in Christ. Living in Christ means you don't make choices without consulting him. Living in Christ means you look to Jesus as your guide through life. There is supernatural power when we go where he tells us and when we do what he tells us to do.

THE TAKEAWAY: If God created the heavens and the earth, there is not one single thing he can't do.

MAY 19TH

Psalm 32:7—"You are my hiding place; you will protect me from trouble and surround me with songs of deliverance."

We have to face up to our mistakes and any other issues that occur in our lives every day. We face our mistakes and the problems of life by hiding in God. I want you to hear that again: we handle our opposition from the enemy by hiding in God. This verse says that once we have hidden in God, he will protect us from trouble. Not only that, but we will be surrounded with songs of deliverance. Therefore, whatever you are facing today, don't run from the problems, but face the problem by hiding in God.

THE TAKEAWAY: Would you like to unleash the presence of God in your life? If the answer is yes, begin to worship God right now.

MAY 20TH

Exodus 14:14—"The Lord will fight for you; you need only to be still."

Stop fighting a battle you weren't meant to fight. If you want to get worn out and tired quickly, try to fight a battle you were not supposed to fight. God wants you and me to let him fight for us. Yes! God wants to fight our battles for us. He desires for us to have his victory and power in our lives, but we can't have it if we do the fighting. We only get his power when we are still. Would you be still before God? That means not giving into worry, fear, doubt, or panic. Friend, God wants you and me to be still so he can fight for us, and most importantly, so that he can win our battles. What a great God!

THE TAKEAWAY: Where are you fighting your own battles, and how is that working out for you? It is difficult at times, but try to take your hands off your problems and turn your hands to God in stillness.

MAY 21ST

Matthew 3:17—"This is my Son, whom I love; with him I am well pleased."

Today's verse was said at the baptism of Jesus. The baptism takes place before Jesus has healed one person. Before he has raised someone from the dead. Before he fed the thousands. Before he accomplished one thing in his ministry! What does this mean? It means God was pleased with Jesus before he ever performed one miracle. He was pleased with him not because of what he did but because of whose he was. How does this relate to you and me? God loves you unconditionally and he is well pleased with you regardless of what you do or don't do. Our culture bases love off performance, but not God. Even when you mess up or say something you shouldn't have said, you are still his. Regardless of what mistakes you make, he loves you because you are his son or daughter. If your faith is in Jesus, you are his and he is pleased.

THE TAKEAWAY: God's love for you is not determined on how you perform in this life. Rest in the fact that God loves you as you are.

MAY 22ND

Psalm 36:9—"For with you is the fountain of life."

The word *fountain* means place of refreshment or source of existence. As you go through today, if you need strength, there will be limited resources if you turn to anyone or anything other than God. When we seek to be fulfilled, only God can satisfy the deepest longings of our hearts. It is only when we turn to God and let him supply refreshment that we have true strength. God is the one who makes our lives truly worth living, so when our hearts are totally turned over to him as our source of all strength, then we have unquenchable love, perfect peace, and a rest that can't be stopped.

THE TAKEAWAY: Alone time with God will do more for your soul than any vacation, spa treatment, or getaway. Get alone with him today.

MAY 23RD

Psalm 37:3—"Trust in the Lord and do good; dwell in the land and enjoy safe pasture."

God wants you to enjoy safe pasture. He wants you to enjoy life. You might be thinking, you don't know what trials I am facing right now. I don't, but God does. The key to enjoying life is walking with God daily. When we are walking, every so often we can get a rock in our shoe. Sometimes over the course of a walk we have to sit down and rest. Just know today that you aren't walking alone, and you aren't walking with someone who doesn't know where to go.

THE TAKEAWAY: The only way to guarantee you won't get God's very best for your life is to stop walking. Keep being faithful to God, and watch how he works things out in your life.

MAY 24TH

2 Chronicles 6:4—"Praise be to the Lord, the God of Israel, who with his hands has fulfilled what he promised with his mouth."

I love how real the Bible is. Don't you wish all people did what they said they would do? Wouldn't it be nice if our leaders were as faithful to their word as God is? What a blessing it would be if all our friends were like this verse? God did what he said he would do. How many times have we heard promises that we knew would never get fulfilled? The good news is every single promise God has made he will fulfill.

THE TAKEAWAY: God's delay does not mean God's denial. Sometimes, God makes us wait for the promise. Hang in there; God will be faithful to what he promised!

MAY 25TH

Psalm 37:4—"Take delight in the Lord, and he will give you the desires of your heart."

God wants you to be fulfilled! God wants you to have so much joy, you can't stand it. However, there is a difference between temporary happiness and joy that lasts, even during the most challenging of times. When we make choices that are self-centered, most times, those choices bring a brief time of happiness followed by regret and pain. God wants us to have a joy that is unstoppable. How do we get that? Delight yourself in the Lord. Delighting ourselves in the Lord can be defined as making God our first and most valuable priority. When God is first, others are second, and we are third; the process of delighting ourselves in the Lord has started.

THE TAKEAWAY: In the eyes of man, putting others before ourselves doesn't seem wise. In the kingdom of God, putting others before ourselves is the pathway to delight!

MAY 26TH

Psalm 42:11—"Why, my soul, are you downcast? Why so disturbed within me? Put your hope in God, for I will yet praise him, my Savior and my God."

How are you? Is it well with your soul? Chances are you might be hanging in there, but is there some issue nagging at you? Perhaps not overwhelmingly, but something that is just annoying. Maybe this day you have something major. Either way, God is asking you and me some questions. Why are you downcast, O my soul? Why so disturbed within me? He is asking those questions because he is with you, he is for you, and because he loves you. So, throughout this day and week when you face something that is stopping you from enjoying life, say this in your mind or out loud, "God is bigger." I promise he really is!

THE TAKEAWAY: When we compare our problems to ourselves, those problems seem big. When we compare our problems to God, those same problems are actually small.

MAY 27TH

Galatians 3:9—"So those who rely on faith are blessed along with Abraham, the man of faith."

Friend, you are blessed. The question is, do you know it? If you want to be blessed, you must have faith that things can change. Faith is believing in what you hope for and what you can't see with your eye. Today, I want to encourage you to have faith that your job will get better. Have faith your relationships can go deeper. Have faith that whatever would hinder your life will be changed. If the devil can get you to stop believing and trusting God the battle is over! God is a God who blesses, and we don't have to be perfect to be blessed. We just need to turn to God in faith.

THE TAKEAWAY: You will never find any place in the Bible that says you have to be perfect to be blessed.

MAY 28TH

Romans 5:20—"Where sin increased, grace increased all the more."

Have you ever let the trash build up in your garage? When this happens, the place begins to stink. So it is with our lives. When we let the trash build up—trash of lies we have told, people we have hurt, mistakes we have made—it makes our attitudes and lives stink. The Bible gives us a great piece of news from Romans 5:20. Friend, we are not able to fix our mistakes, but if we give them to God, he will. Imagine the more mistakes and sins that are made, the more grace God then provides. What a good and loving God we serve.

THE TAKEAWAY: No matter what we do, forgiveness can never be achieved. Forgiveness can only be received.

MAY 29TH

Galatians 5:1—"It was for freedom that Christ has set us free."

Today, God wants you free. Yes, today! God wants you free from guilt, low self-esteem, anger, fear, doubt, worry, and depression. You name it, God wants you free. The only thing we are not to be free from is love. For those who call themselves believers, we are to be bound in love to God and one another. God wants you to have an Independence Day. Whatever you have done, Jesus has set you free. Therefore, if God says you are free, then you are free. Step out and walk in freedom. Let go of the past, the hurts, the pain, the harsh memories, and stop trying to understand everything that has happened in your life.

THE TAKEAWAY: The past can only poison the future if we allow it to do so.

MAY 30TH

Galatians 6:9—"Let us not become weary in doing good, for at the proper time we will reap a harvest if we do not give up."

The message is simple, don't give up. God wants to encourage you to keep going. Keep doing what is right, even if those around you don't see you doing right. Why? Because maybe not today, but sometime, you will reap a harvest. Don't give up on your marriage, dream, project, child, friendship, or whatever is in your heart. Friend, many times we are tempted to throw in the towel, but don't do it. God has huge plans for your life, and the devil can't touch them, so he will try to get you to give up. Don't listen to his lies.

THE TAKEAWAY: If the devil can't keep you from dreaming, he will do everything he can to get you to give up on your dreams.

MAY 31ST

Ephesians 1:11—"In him we were also chosen."

I hope this one thought stays in your mind all day long. God chose you! One more time, God chose you. God sees all your warts, wrinkles, mistakes, and yet, he chose you. He sees all my sins and mistakes and yet he still chose me. How does that apply to us today? When we feel down, he chose us. When we hurt someone, he chose us. When we do things that we know we will regret, he chose us. God's love for you and me is not performance based; no, it is position based. Our position in life is we are the chosen of God. Should we love others, should we help people, should we be pure, yes! But when we fail, he still chose us! If you get down, don't stay there; you are chosen by God!

THE TAKEAWAY: Low self-esteem is based on how we feel those we value look at us. God chose you, so you shouldn't have low self-esteem. The creator of the world chose you!

JUNE 1ST

Ephesians 1:7-8—"In accordance with the riches of God's grace that he lavished on us."

What a thought! Lavish doesn't simply mean to give only to meet the need. Lavish means to provide more than what is needed or required. God wants to give us more grace than is needed or required. Wow! So, when you get stressed or life gets overwhelming, take a few moments and remember that no matter what you face in life, God has given us more love and more grace than we need!

THE TAKEAWAY: God gives us an overflow of his grace but not just for us alone. God gives us an abundance of his grace so we have a portion to give away to others.

JUNE 2ND

John 8:26—"But he who sent me is trustworthy."

A while back my wife and I flew out of town to perform a wedding for a friend of mine. As I did the ceremony, it was apparent God brought this couple together. God didn't bring the couple together because they were seeking each other. God brought the couple together because they were seeking him first. Friend, when you seek God first, he will provide for all of your needs as well as the desires in your heart.

THE TAKEAWAY: If you are worried about whether God will come through in an area of your life, you are wasting time. With God, his reliability is 100%.

JUNE 3RD

Philippians 2:14—"Do everything without grumbling or arguing."

God is working in you, through you, and for you. However, there are times that we can slow God's hand that is at work in us. How do we do that? By complaining or arguing. When we grumble and argue about all the problems we are facing, we are not fixing those issues, but we are possibly making those problems worse. A complaint is noise that everyone hears and nobody cares about. There is power in quietly trusting God.

THE TAKEAWAY: God gave you two ears and one mouth. That means we are supposed to listen twice as much as we speak.

JUNE 4TH

Philippians 3:13—"But one thing I do: Forgetting what is behind and straining toward what is ahead."

Let it go! Forget it! Move on! Perhaps today you are holding on to unforgiveness because someone has done something to hurt you. Jesus paid it all. He paid for our sins, he paid for our hurts, and he paid for the sins of those who sin against us. Today let go of your sin and hurt. Release and let go of other people's mistakes toward you. When you hold on to the past, you lose the future. Don't forfeit your blessing by holding on to something from the past.

THE TAKEAWAY: A believer can only go so far as his or her ability to let go of the past.

JUNE 5TH

Phil 3:21—"By the power that enables him to bring everything under his control."

Have you ever felt powerless? God gives us a huge promise here. He has the power to bring everything under his control. Wow! That means any relationship, money situation, job, family member, or fear can be brought under his control. When we feel like we have lost all control in our lives, God can still bring it under his control. Therefore, don't give up hope. In fact, God wants you to get your hopes up. No matter what might seem hopeless, he can bring it under control, and he will, if you surrender it to him.

THE TAKEAWAY: Remember you can't control what others do but you can control what you do.

JUNE 6TH

1 Corinthians 16:13—"Be on your guard; stand firm in the faith."

Stand firm. Sometimes instead of standing we want to run. Or perhaps instead of standing firm we want to sit the battle out. Friend, there is so much power in just standing firm. We are all tempted at the first sight of trouble to run or give up. Stand firm in your calling. Stand firm on God's Word. Stand firm in your commitments. Stand firm on your principles. Stand firm in God.

THE TAKEAWAY: Nothing is impossible with men and women who have the guts to stand firm and be counted as followers of Christ. Stand firm.

JUNE 7TH

1 Timothy 1:16—"Christ Jesus might display his immense patience as an example for those who would believe in him and receive eternal life."

What I love about God is he can easily do what I struggle to do. What I love is he is patient with me. Too many times, people see God as a demanding Father. The Word of God teaches that he is a loving God who is patient with his children. Today, if you're struggling to be patient with yourself or others, ask God to give to you from his limitless supply. And just maybe you are being too hard on yourself. If God has patience for you, maybe you should cut yourself and others some slack. He loves you just as you are!

THE TAKEAWAY: This old phrase is so true, "Haste makes waste." Be patient with God and his promises.

JUNE 8TH

Romans 4:8—"Blessed is the man whose sin the Lord will never count against them."

Who's counting? Have you heard that phrase before? I know of two people who count our sins, mistakes and failures. First the devil does and secondly many times we do. Let me ask you: Where have you tripped up lately? Where have you stumbled? If you can answer that question quickly, chances are you might be holding on to your mistakes too closely. God is more concerned with where we are going than with where we have been.

THE TAKEAWAY: Don't bring up what God isn't counting.

JUNE 9TH

Psalm 85:8—"He promises peace to his people."

Peace is in high demand. With government elections, the economy, and all the business that is in our lives, peace is needed. Today, I want to encourage you that God promises peace. He doesn't promise that the person we want to get elected will be elected. He doesn't promise that our nation's economy will be perfect. He doesn't promise that once you receive the love of God everything will go perfectly with your life. However, he does make a promise to give you peace. If you are troubled today, I invite you to accept the peace of God. Rest in God. Verbally lay your concerns at his feet and rest. When God gives you a promise, you can take it to the bank!

THE TAKEAWAY: What are you feeding your mind? Put a filter on your mind and let it be fed with the Word of God.

JUNE 10TH

2 Timothy 1:7—"For the Spirit God gave us does not make us timid, but gives us power, love and self-discipline."

Don't be afraid! God does not want you to have fear anywhere in your heart. God wants you to receive his gifts of power, love, and self-discipline. Today, if life has thrown you a curve ball, if you read the news and are nervous, if someone or something has put some fear in your heart, release it. Don't try to understand it, don't negotiate with it, but release it to God.

THE TAKEAWAY: It doesn't take a lot of man if God has all the man. The degree to which you give God control of your life will determine how much power you have.

JUNE 11TH

2 Timothy 2:1—"Be strong in the grace that is in Christ Jesus."

Be strong. How can we be strong? By focusing on the grace that is in Jesus. What does that mean? Have you ever worked for a demanding boss where you feel pressure to be perfect? You may feel like you have to do everything exactly right. Does God want us to do things right? Yes! Does God want us to aim for excellence? Yes! However, with God, when we don't measure up, when we lose control, when we make mistakes, we have strength because God's grace covers over our messes. Therefore friend, receive the strength of Jesus through the grace of Jesus.

THE TAKEAWAY: God isn't demanding of us. Is there someone in your life you have been demanding of where perhaps you need to show him or her the grace of Jesus?

JUNE 12TH

Genesis 1:1—"In the beginning God created the heavens and the earth."

The truth is God created everything. He is the boss. He is not the president or prime minister, but he is the ruler of the world. He also happens to be a loving Father. If God knows all things and created everything, perhaps we need to make sure he is our main counselor. In whatever place life finds you today, make sure you're not just doing something and then asking God to bless it. Ask God what he will bless and then start doing it.

THE TAKEAWAY: Have you taken a moment to ask God what he will bless before you start doing it?

JUNE 13TH

Nehemiah 2:20—"The God of heaven will give us success."

I love succeeding and I hate failing. However, in all our lives, we have done both. Notice that God is the giver of success. Have you ever done everything right, yet still did not succeed? These three mistakes can keep us from receiving the success that God wants us to receive from him:

1) Becoming impatient and settling for less than God's best.
2) Doing all the work without first asking him what should be done.
3) Believing success is up to us.

Friend, God wants to give you success, but it is he who gives success. Your boss, your company, or your own hands can't give you that success, only God can!

THE TAKEAWAY: Success in life isn't about pleasing man. Success in life is about pleasing God.

JUNE 14TH

Colossians 4:5—"Make the most of every opportunity."

Most people think small is—well—small. But not God. Throughout the Bible, we see God using the small things in big ways. Every opportunity we encounter in life gives us the possibility to do something amazing. With God, little is much when it is in his hands. Read that one more time: with God, little is much when it is in his hands.

THE TAKEAWAY: Today, examine your world and ask God to open your eyes to the opportunities that are all around you. Oftentimes, the greatest opportunities are right in front of us; they are called trials.

JUNE 15TH

Psalm 91:15—"I will be with him in trouble."

Have you ever had people in your life who were only friends with you when you had money, when you had a job, when you had the nice house, or when you were highly successful? Have you seen those same so-called friends leave when you were without money, power, position, or influence? Today, God makes a promise to be with us in trouble. It blesses my heart that God commits to being right in the middle of our messes with us. Thank God he is with us during the good and tough times.

THE TAKEAWAY: The only way to get out of trouble is to invite God into your trials. Are you facing troubles on your own or have you invited God into the mess?

JUNE 16TH

Psalm 98:1—"He has done marvelous things."

God has done amazing things! He has allowed us to live. He has allowed us to be citizens in a free country. He has allowed us to hear about his love. Today, don't let the enemy get you in the trap of dwelling on things you do not have. Could things be better? Maybe. Could we have more time with our families? Maybe. Could we have more money? Sure. But friend, the enemy always tries to get us focused on what we don't have, and God always tries to get us focused on what we do have. When we begin thanking God every day, we become stronger, deeper, and more powerful.

THE TAKEAWAY: If you made a list of blessings, what would be on the list? Maybe you should make one today.

JUNE 17TH

Ephesians 6:10—"Finally, be strong in the Lord and in his mighty power."

Today, you can be strong! The Bible says, "Be strong in the Lord." Friend, we can be resilient not because of us but because of God. Are you trying to be strong on your own? Today, examine your life and the areas where you are trying to move in your own strength, and give those areas to God. His strength alone knows no equal. If you feel powerless or helpless, that isn't the final word. The final word is that we get God's power because we are his children. Today, we can either fail in our own power or overcome in his.

THE TAKEAWAY: Strength cannot be measured in the victories of life; strength can only be measured in trials.

JUNE 18TH

Philippians 4:13—"I can do all this through him who gives me strength."

Do you want a shot of excitement? Here it is - I can do all things. The devil will attempt to lie to you about that statement. He wants you to hear you can't get that job, you can't go back to school, you won't achieve that honor, and the list goes on and on. Friend, God has no limits and he wants you to understand that you can do all things. So, today, remove the limits. Stop accepting second best in your life. You can do all things. Start declaring it, start thinking it, and start living it.

THE TAKEAWAY: You are more powerful than you think you are! Think about it.

JUNE 19TH

Hebrews 9:14—"Offered himself unblemished to God, cleanse our consciences."

Have you ever struggled with guilt and couldn't shake it? Guilt for a lie, mistake, or something hidden that nobody knew about? Friend, God provided the answer: Jesus sacrifice. There is no way to remove guilt by ourselves. If there is something you can't shake, realize you will never be able to do so on your own. But once you ask God to forgive you, not only is that sin paid for, but also it is removed. We can sleep and live in peace because God is the one who did the cleaning in our lives, not us.

THE TAKEAWAY: As long as we are alive, we will struggle with and be tempted by sin. However, the answer is never found in us, it is only found in Jesus and his sacrifice for us.

JUNE 20TH

Nehemiah 13:2—"Our God, however, turned the curse into a blessing."

Only God can do what the above verse says. God can turn what we think is a low point in our life and make it into something great. Today, what is in your life that you want or need God to turn around? What seems to be a curse or a pain in your side? God can turn that pain and make it a blessing. So, don't give in to the pity party. Realize God specializes in making what seems to us to be a problem and he makes it something wonderful. Right now, ask God to bring to your mind what is causing you pain and then let him turn it into a blessing!

THE TAKEAWAY: The only way God can't turn a curse into a blessing is if we don't let him.

JUNE 21ST

Hebrews 11:34—"Whose weakness was turned to strength."

Wow! Turning my weakness into a strength is a serious miracle. For me, that means overeating, my lack of patience, and watching sports can become a strength? With God, Yes. You might say, "How?" Well, that is a great question. All I do know is that once we acknowledge what our weaknesses are and submit those to God, he does the rest. For example, with overeating: he turned this weakness into a strength and helped me lose over fifty pounds and keep it off, which in turn helped me to assist others to do the same. Today, wherever you are weak, God can help you become strong. Identify those areas and give them to God. God has huge plans for your life!

THE TAKEAWAY: Weakness becomes strength in God's hands.

JUNE 22ND

Hebrews 12:1—"Let us run with perseverance."

Today, are you running in life or walking? Are you living every minute to its fullest or are you in a place where you can't wait for the day to be finished? Friend, God wants you to run, enjoy and be excited about your life. If something is trying to drag you down and you don't think you can survive it, I encourage you to persevere. Persevere means to continue steadfastly. Don't give up or give in today. Don't quit on your dreams and desires. God wants you to win in life!

THE TAKEAWAY: What is it going to take for you to persevere? Just consider that you can't win in any area of life without perseverance.

JUNE 23RD

Psalm 91:11—"For he will command his angels concerning you to guard you in all your ways."

In my life, I have flipped a car and truck upside down, been thrown from a horse, been in a plane for an emergency landing, and have escaped a motorcycle accident. What is my point? For some of you, it is probably, "I better not use any form of transportation with Barry." However, the main point is this: turning to God is the only safe place in our lives. Friend, God can give you safety in your job, marriage, and in every area of life. Today, realize God loves you and rest in his protection. Don't live your life being scared or in constant fear, but instead remember that God is your protector.

THE TAKEAWAY: You can only fear what hasn't been yielded to God.

JUNE 24TH

Romans 8:37—"No, in all these things we are more than conquerors through him who loved us."

Today God wants you to conquer. He wants you to conquer that fear, low self-esteem issue, or that bad habit. He wants you to triumph over whatever you might be facing that is trying to bring your life down. We all face what appear to be giants in our lives. However, God desires that we would be a conqueror. Notice that we can't do those things in our own power, but it is "through him who loved us." So, don't give into the thought that you can't do this or you can't do that. With God, you can do all things!

THE TAKEAWAY: Another word for a conqueror is *champion*. You might not feel like or think you look like a champion. However, if you are a believer in Christ you are more than a conqueror!

JUNE 25TH

Psalm 105:41—"He opened the rock, and water gushed out."

I know the above verse might not immediately say much to you. However, look closer. God opened a rock. I don't know about you, but I don't have the power, knowledge, or strength to just open up a rock. And I sure don't know how to make water gush out. What is the point? This act is something only God could do. We will wear ourselves out if we try to do what only God can do. Are you trying to put a relationship back together? Are you trying to find your dream job? Are you looking for the perfect spouse? Friend, we need to do what we can do and rest and then let God do what only he can do. This day, don't wear yourself out trying to do what only God can do. Take a deep breath and give him what is stressing, troubling, or causing you unrest.

THE TAKEAWAY: God brought refreshment out of nowhere. Believe God to bring your soul refreshing from unlikely places.

JUNE 26TH

Esther 4:14—"That you have come to your royal position for such a time as this?"

This verse speaks about Queen Esther and the position that God had for her at that time. God placed her in that royal position for a reason. Today, wherever you are and whatever you are doing, God has you there for a purpose and a reason! You might be looking to work another job, you might want another home, or you might want to relocate to another city. And perhaps that is God's will; however, today you are where you are at for a reason. A professor of mine once said, "Bloom where you are planted." As you go through this day, don't let your focus be about how the grass could be greener on the other side of the fence; think about how God has blessed you and know God has a plan for you today.

THE TAKEAWAY: You don't have an ordinary life. You are a believer in Jesus and therefore you have an extraordinary life.

JUNE 27TH

Psalm 62:5—"Yes, my soul, find rest in God."

You deserve some rest. Not just sleep, but also rest. Have you ever woken up from your sleep and still been tired? We are all holding on to things that can make our inner soul churn with pain, fear or anxiety. No amount of money, sports, shopping, eating, can calm our inner self. Today, rest in the fact that those who call on the Lord are his children. Rest in the fact that God is in control. Rest in the fact that you are fearfully and wonderfully made, and God is not through with your life.

THE TAKEAWAY: Sometimes if we don't watch it, we can wear ourselves out trying to get rest. There is no greater form of rest than to truly get alone in the presence of God.

JUNE 28TH

Psalm 107:43—"Ponder the loving deeds of the Lord."

Monday is coming, if not today, someday. Back to work, back to the daily grind, back to a schedule. Today, as you might be facing the fast pace of life let me encourage you to consider the loving deeds of the Lord. I want to challenge you throughout your day to just ponder where God has been good to you. As you drive, have meetings, and face stress, think about how much God loves you. You are the object of God's love; isn't that good news?

THE TAKEAWAY: The true value of any object is solely based on what the owner is willing to pay. God loved you so much he was willing to pay with his Son's life so he could be in relationship with you.

JUNE 29TH

Philippians 1:3—"I thank my God every time I remember you."

You can be greedy or you can be thankful, but you can't be both. Every day should be Thanksgiving. We need to daily thank God for the gift of his love, his Son, and the life he has given to us. We need to thank those in our lives who bless us. Friend, we have a choice: we can be givers or takers. I promise you, givers enjoy their lives way more and have significantly less regrets than takers. Be blessed, and Happy Thanksgiving in June!

THE TAKEAWAY: What are you whining and complaining about? Instead of grumbling, begin to thank God for what you do have. You will be amazed how your day just changed!

JUNE 30TH

John 4:50—"The man took Jesus at his word and departed."

My prayer for you and me is that we would actually take Jesus at his word and believe him. I pray that we would actually trust what God and his Word says about us as the full truth. The Bible says, "The man took Jesus at his word." In others words, he believed God and went on his way without doubting. Today, the Word says:

> You are healed (Psalm 103:3).
> You are forgiven (1 John 1:9).
> You can do anything (Luke 1:37).
> You are loved (John 3:16).
> You have an amazing life adventure ahead of you (Jeremiah 29:11).

Today, believe it, receive it, and depart knowing it!

THE TAKEAWAY: God said it, so that settles it.

JULY 1ST

John 5:24—"Whoever hears my word and believes him who sent me has eternal life."

Do you see the power of belief? Believing or faith in God connects us to God. There is power in belief! Let me give you three truths about faith:

1) Believes the improbable.
2) Moves the immovable.
3) Receives the impossible.

Today, don't stop believing God for your life! No matter how big your requests, don't stop asking God. He believes in you, you should believe in him!

THE TAKEAWAY: The greatest obstacle to seeing the supernatural power of God at work in our lives is our lack of faith.

JULY 2ND

John 7:24—"Stop judging by mere appearances, but instead judge correctly."

You have heard the phrase; "You can't judge a book by its cover." This state-ment is so true. Today, I want to encourage you not to only look at the outer appearance. Maybe someone in your life is causing you a lot of grief. Perhaps that person is in your life so God can use you to bring healing to his or her heart. Maybe there is a job offer that just doesn't seem to be a good one, but that could be the job that gives you a crucial contact. Maybe there is a struggle in your life that God could use to give you insight that could give hope to millions. I want to challenge you today: don't look at people, jobs, or problems simply as they are. God wants to bless you, and many times he will use what we don't think appears to be important to do so.

THE TAKEAWAY: Have you lost focus? We can only have the right focus on our lives when we try to see things God's way.

JULY 3RD

Psalm 113:7—"He raises the poor from the dust and lifts the needy from the ash heap."

Do you need a lift today? God wants to raise you up. This verse says, "He raises the poor." Do you need some encouragement? Let the following thoughts sink in:

1) God is for you (Jeremiah 29:11).
2) God is with you (Joshua 1:5).
3) God wants to protect you (Exodus 14:14).
4) God can turn anything around in your life (Philippians 4:13).

If you need a lift today, God can do it and will do it if you will submit to him!

THE TAKEAWAY: Sometimes, we put the right energy into the wrong area, which will always wear us out. Ask God to direct you on where to pour out your energy.

JULY 4TH

2 Chronicles 7:14—"If my people, who are called by my name, will humble themselves and pray and seek my face and turn from their wicked ways, then I will hear from heaven and I will forgive their sin and will heal their land."

Our nation and its people need healing. The enemy is not the Democrats or the Republicans. The enemy is Satan. We need to honor our fellow Americans who we disagree with, yet still follow our principles. Every American needs to vote, but ultimately, only God and not the government can heal people's hearts and lives. Pray for God to guide our country today.

THE TAKEAWAY: Your prayers and actions can change the world! Believe and start making a difference.

JULY 5TH

Psalm 115:17—"It is not the dead who praise the Lord."

You might be thinking, why are we beginning the day with this type of verse? Notice the Bible says, "It is not the dead who praise the Lord." Look at the key word, *dead*. If you are reading this, you are alive. Today, God wants you to live a blessed life. He wants his dreams for you to become reality. God can use your life and do things with it you never imagined. Don't let another day pass without believing, asking, and starting to live life on the offensive. No matter what you are going through, today you are alive and today is a gift, so praise the Lord!

THE TAKEAWAY: What is one thing you can do today that will change not only your life but also somebody else's?

JULY 6TH

John 13:5—"After that, he poured water into a basin and began to wash his disciples' feet."

Today's verse is the example for all of us. Just as Jesus washed feet, we are to do so as well. That means we are to serve and help those who God has placed in our lives. Today, I want to encourage you to look for someone you can bless. Look for someone who seems to have a need, whether small or large, and meet it today. Serving others is a powerful message from this verse, but also don't lose sight that it was the Lord who poured the water. This day, Jesus wants to wash your feet. Maybe you need him to wash away a sin, done. (Psalm 103:3). Maybe you need him to wash away a bad attitude, done. (Col. 3:2). Maybe today you need him to wash away discouragement or pain, done. (Psalm 147:3). Friend, God is for you; let him minister to you today.

THE TAKEAWAY: There is a supernatural act that takes place when we serve others. For some reason, blessing others blesses us.

JULY 7TH

1 John 4:4—"The one who is in you is greater than the one who is in the world."

The verse today teaches those who believe, "The one who is in you is greater than the one who is in the world." Greatness is inside of you, but the key is we all have to let it out. Sometimes we keep that greatness locked up inside of us because of fear, or peer pressure, or we just want to go with the flow. Friend, this day the truth is the power of God is in you, and we can live in God's blessings if we simply let it out!

THE TAKEAWAY: What tries to hinder you from letting out the life of God in your life?

JULY 8TH

John 14:27—"Peace I leave with you."

Jesus is speaking to you today. He not only wants you to hear this word but to receive it, "Peace I leave with you." I love the fact that Jesus, the Prince of Peace, grants us peace in many ways like giving a Christmas present. Is your heart filled with anxiety? Can you sleep? Does your mind wander about things that bring you pain or worry? If you answer yes to any of those three questions, I ask you to receive the gift of peace from Jesus. Sometimes people take presents but never get around to opening them. Give yourself a break today by opening up and receiving the peace of Jesus knowing that whatever is going on today, God loves you and he is in control.

THE TAKEAWAY: Give into the peace of Jesus.

JULY 9TH

Ephesians 6:19—"I will fearlessly make known the mystery of the gospel."

Are your surviving or thriving in life? God has called you to thrive in this life! Oftentimes, what keeps us from thriving, however, is fear. Fear of what others will think, fear of failing, or fear of the unknown can stop us in our tracks. My brother was successful at everything he did because he lived a fearless life. Friend, if you want an abundant life, kick fear out!

THE TAKEAWAY: Not giving in to fear is what separates good from great. What are you giving into?

JULY 10TH

Psalm 53:6—"When God restores his people."

Have you lost something of value? Perhaps a valuable coin, picture, or maybe even a relationship? God makes a promise in this verse that no other person or power on earth can make. God promises to restore the blessings and fortunes of his people. Don't buy into the lie of the devil that something in your life can't be restored. Instead, buy into the truth that God is able and will restore your life.

THE TAKEAWAY: God does new things in our lives when we have a new mindset. Put on the mindset that God can and will restore what has been lost or stolen!

JULY 11TH

Luke 22:50-51—"And one of them struck the servant of the high priest, cutting off his right ear. But Jesus answered, 'No more of this!' And he touched the man's ear and healed him."

At this point in the story, Jesus is being arrested and is about to begin the process that would lead to his crucifixion. Even though this is a stressful time, he performs another expression of his love. Notice the Bible says, "And one of them struck the servant." That one who struck and cut off the ear of the high priest's servant was Peter. Then, Jesus miraculously heals the man's ear. The greatest miracle is not that the ear was put back on, but that Jesus saved Peter from imprisonment or death. Had Jesus not have mended the ear of the servant, Peter could have been charged with attempted murder and possibly be put to death for his actions. Jesus saved Peter from the results of his sinful misstep and he still does this for us today. If you have made a mistake in your marriage, or with your job, or in your private life, I want you to receive this word. If Jesus can literally put someone's ear back, he can heal your life from any sinful action you make. No wonder they call him the savior!

THE TAKEAWAY: You cannot fix your past, but God can!

JULY 12TH

1 John 4:4—"The one who is in you is greater than the one who is in the world."

Once you have connected with God through Jesus Christ, you have his power. You might not be able to see God's power. You might not be able to feel God's power. Friend, walking in the power of God has nothing to do with your feelings. Walking in the power of God has everything to do with the truth. The truth is no matter what is against you, the power of God in you is greater than what you might be facing.

THE TAKEAWAY: Often times the most powerful forces in this world cannot be seen by the human eye.

JULY 13TH

Psalm 103:10—"He does not treat us as our sins deserve."

This promise is remarkable! When we should get what we deserve concerning our sins and mistakes, God chooses in his love not to treat us accordingly. Friend, Jesus paid the heavy price for our sins and took the punishment we deserve and in turn, gave us what we don't deserve, his amazing grace! We can exchange our sorrow for God's healing. We can give him our confusion for his wisdom. We can bring him our failings and receive his strength and power.

THE TAKEAWAY: Have you truly considered the many things God has spared you from? The next time you are asked how you are doing, consider saying, "Better than I deserve."

JULY 14TH

Psalm 18:29—"With your help I can advance against a troop; with my God I can scale a wall."

Do you know that God is in your corner? This verse states that with God you can advance against an army and overcome barriers. Perhaps you feel as though there is an army of depression or financial problems against you. Maybe you feel as if there is a wall you can't climb such as a wall that represents a promotion or an issue in your family or personal life? No matter what you are facing today, God can and will help you overcome it.

THE TAKEAWAY: What enemy to your life's destiny do you need to overcome? When you face it, remember that you are not alone because God is with you!

JULY 15TH

Psalm 119:156—"Your compassion, Lord, is great."

Do you know what the word *compassion* means? Compassion is feeling sympathy for someone to the extent you take action to help them. It is simple to just say words like I love you or I like you. But beyond mere words and lip service, we show compassion and love for one another when we are moved to take action and do something to help a person in distress. As you start your day, remember that God is moved with compassion to act on your behalf. The creator of this world has his heart set on you.

THE TAKEAWAY: God always has compassion for you. Today, ask God to help you have compassion for someone who is in need of your help.

JULY 16TH

Job 19:25—"I know that my Redeemer lives."

Knowing that your Redeemer lives is a key to enjoying life. For those who do not believe in God, there is no hope in hopeless situations, there is no peace in the storms of life, and there is no strength to be found when everything is against you. But good news, Jesus is alive and he loves you just as you are. So, the next time you are in a tough spot, just think or say out loud, "I know my Redeemer lives," and let the truth of his life affect your life. God is for you!

THE TAKEAWAY: If Jesus overcame death, hell, and the grave, he can help you overcome any storm in your life.

JULY 17TH

Psalm 121:1-2—"I lift up my eyes to the mountains—where does my help come from? My help comes from the Lord, the maker of heaven and earth."

Today, where do you need help? There are times in our attempts to give and serve those around us, where we ourselves grow weary and our emotional tanks become empty. We find ourselves burning the candle at both ends and being in need of help. If we are not careful, we can find ourselves turning to the wrong source for our help when we are emotionally run down. God has already turned to you and me out of his great unconditional love for us. Today, take your eyes off of the stressors that are draining you and put them on the One who promises to deliver you.

THE TAKEAWAY: There is power in focus. A laser is simply focused light. Put your focus on the Lord not your challenges and see how he reaches out to help you.

JULY 18TH

Job 22:23—"If you return to the Almighty, you will be restored."

Have you ever had a relationship stolen or a dream dashed? This verse is one of the many reasons God is so good. To restore means to return. God can return what the devil has robbed from you. God can return your peace of mind, your hope, a job, or anything else the devil has attempted to steal from you. Today, don't let what you don't have burden you; let what God will return to you excite you!

THE TAKEAWAY: The enemy is constantly trying to confuse us, and he is always lying to us. If God says he will restore, don't let any power on earth move you off of that truth.

JULY 19TH

1 John 2:1—"But if anybody does sin, we have an advocate with the Father— Jesus Christ, the Righteous One."

Sometimes when we make mistakes, we feel as though Jesus won't want anything to do with us. No! It is quite the contrary. If you are a believer, when you sin, Jesus will speak up for you. Jesus will defend you. And most importantly, Jesus has already paid in full the penalty for your sin with his own life. You have the power to say no to temptation, but when you don't, you have a loving Savior who will come to your side as your loving defense attorney.

THE TAKEAWAY: The next time you mess up, consider this truth: you don't drown by falling in the water; you drown by staying in it.

JULY 20TH

Psalm 124:8—"Our help is in the name of the Lord."

There are many different names for God. Some short, some long. The Bible offers a variety of ways to call out to God. Here are a few: Savior, Healer, Counselor, King, Lord, Friend, Prince of Peace, Father, Daddy, and Almighty. You might ask, why does God have so many different names for himself? Well, at times we need a savior from our troubles. When we are confused or broken-hearted, we need a counselor. Sometimes we need a friend when those we trust have left us. The good news today is our help is in the name of the Lord and he freely gives to his children.

THE TAKEAWAY: The name of Jesus has power to move mountains and restore lives!

JULY 21ST

Psalm 125:2—"As the mountains surround Jerusalem, so the Lord surrounds his people both now and forevermore."

When have you been in a jam? Surrounded by trouble or pain on all sides? The Bible puts a twist on being surrounded. This verse gives us a huge promise that the Lord surrounds his people both now and forevermore. There are two things God wants us to understand from this verse. First of all, no matter what we are facing, God is surrounding us and wants to protect and prosper us. Secondly, not only is he protecting us today but he will continue doing so forever. What a promise! Friend, as you go about your day, know that you are surrounded and your life is in good hands.

THE TAKEAWAY: Where do you feel surrounded? Begin to worship God and let the truth that God and not your problems are surrounding you.

JULY 22ND

Acts 10:15—"Do not call anything impure that God has made clean."

Have you ever struggled with having a clean conscience? I know I have. God gives an unbelievable statement here with this verse. Most people know if you go to God and ask him to forgive you for your sins, he will. However, many people don't realize that we are then also clean. If there is not enough evidence to convict someone when he or she goes to trial, the person is declared not guilty. However, the court can also pronounce a declaration of innocence to those who received a not guilty verdict who are truly found to be not guilty and completely innocent of the crime. Good news, when we repent of our sins to God, he not only declares us not guilty, but he also gives us a declaration of innocence.

THE TAKEAWAY: Start talking about yourself the way God talks about you.

JULY 23RD

1 Samuel 17:47—"The battle is the Lord's."

What are you battling today? Is it low self-esteem, guilt, depression, stressors at work or some other Goliath? I don't know what it is, but I do know whatever you are battling, God wants to fight for you. Today, I want to ask you to do something that is very difficult. Stop fighting your already won battles! The Lord wants to fight for you. Many times, I make a bad situation worse because I think I can solve the problem on my own without God's help. God loves you and his plan is to fight that battle for you.

THE TAKEAWAY: Stop fighting battles God hasn't asked you to fight. The issues you are dealing with today belong to God.

JULY 24TH

Psalm 130:1—"Out of the depths I cry to you, Lord."

I remember one day I had a major problem and tried to call my wife. She was out of town and I couldn't get a hold of her; I hated it! However, God was happily waiting on me to turn to him. Notice the Bible says, "Out of the depths I cry to you." No matter where you are: out of town, in town, out of coverage, in coverage, or even in the depths of despair, God hears you and loves you. You are not alone and you never will be! Isn't that amazing news?

THE TAKEAWAY: Do you feel alone? Today, step out in faith and believe that God is right by you side ready to listen to the cries of your heart.

JULY 25TH

Psalm 132:11—"The Lord swore an oath to David, a sure oath he will not revoke."

Things change in this world fast! One political party seems to have power and then it switches and the other has power. Economies flourish one moment and then decline the next moment. One sports team is winning then another starts losing. A lot of things change and change quickly. However, God's promises don't change and neither does he. He promises to forgive us, love us, strengthen us, and never leave us. The promises found throughout the Bible never change. So, as we deal with this ever-changing world we live in; don't forget God and his promises won't change.

THE TAKEAWAY: In our society, we are always focused on contracts. The issue with contracts is often there can be loopholes and it can be easily broken. On the other hand, God makes covenants with his people, which are promises that are never broken and never-ending.

JULY 26TH

Acts 17:28—"For in him we live and move and have our being."

When I get in trouble, I live in me instead of in God. I do what I want. This verse is showing us that, "In him we live and move and have our being." Today, as you go about your day, don't live for yourself, live in and through God. Live in God's love and power. Consider making your choices through the lens of, "What does God want?" Friend, God wants you and me to have an incredible life, but that can only take place when we let him guide us.

THE TAKEAWAY: When we live in him, we will live in blessings. When we live in us, we will live in troubles.

JULY 27TH

Job 38:1—"Then the Lord spoke to Job out of the storm."

I love this verse! We have heard about God answering our prayers, but this goes deeper. This verse is full of exciting news. Notice the Lord answered Job "out of the storm." There are times in all our lives when we get in a storm of depression, anger, unforgiveness or pain. Sometimes these storms last a few minutes, others a few weeks and some longer. God moves in people's hearts and lives not just when they are doing good, but also when the storms of life occur. Friend, God loves you and wants to answer you, even when you are in a storm!

THE TAKEAWAY: God is speaking today, but are you listening? Would you consider spending time with him today just listening for his voice?

JULY 28TH

Proverbs 16:4—"The Lord works out everything to its proper end."

Have you ever let something small affect you like the world was coming to an end? Right now, you might be allowing yourself to feel too busy, too stressed, or too overwhelmed. Friend, let this piece of good news speak to you, "The Lord works out everything." God is in control so that you can enjoy today!

THE TAKEAWAY: What part of everything do you not understand? If God says he will work everything out that means God will work everything out.

JULY 29TH

Luke 1:37—"For no word from God will ever fail."

What do you think is impossible in your life? What is it that you doubt can happen? Do you have trouble believing a relationship can be healed? Do you have difficulty believing that a bill can be paid? Is it hard for you to think about a job situation changing? Friend, God does the impossible— that is why he is called God. I want to encourage you not to give up on something just because you believe it is impossible.

THE TAKEAWAY: How would your life change if the word *impossible* was removed from your vocabulary?

JULY 30TH

Mark 1:27—"He even gives orders to impure spirits and they obey him"

Have you watched a traffic officer? When they raise their hands 3000-pound cars stop. Why do they stop? Does the police officer have superman like power that comes out of them that shuts the engines down or forces the breaks to stop the car? No! Police Officers are able to stop 3000-pound approaching cars because of the authority they carry. Friend, you have more authority than any police badge could ever produce. If you are a follower of Jesus you have the authority of Jesus. So if something isn't going well in your life, today you can take authority over it! You are a child of God and because of what Jesus did on the cross you have access to the authority of the father.

THE TAKEAWAY: Are you walking in the full power that God has given you?

JULY 31ST

Galatians 5:1—"It is for freedom that Christ has set us free."

You are free! What have you struggled to be free from? There are a host of things I could list that we all can wrestle with every day. The good news is that because of the love of God and Jesus's sacrifice, we can be free. How? We get freedom by simply believing that we are free and walking in that truth. Right believing will eventually lead to right living. It is one thing to say you believe; it is another thing to actually live that truth out on a daily basis. Friend, Jesus wants you free, and because he rose from the grave, you are!

THE TAKEAWAY: Right believing will always eventually lead to right living. Freedom is a choice!

AUGUST 1ST

Psalm 46:10—"Be still, and know that I am God."

God asks us to do something that can be so difficult, be still. I don't like to be still. I like to work, move, and get things done. I struggle when I know something needs to be done and I am not doing anything to fix it. Many of the issues you and I face, we can't fix. God wants us to be still so that he can work on the issues. Have you ever seen a father fixing his car and his little son keeps getting in the way? He loves his son, but he needs him to move out of the way so he can fix the car. God loves us, but at times we can get in the way of what God is doing. God knows exactly how to fix the problems in our lives, but when we try to do the fixing, we make it worse. Today, be still.

THE TAKEAWAY: Much of the Christian life is easier said than done. Start with small steps. Small steps every day equal big returns!

AUGUST 2ND

Matthew 7:11—"How much more will your Father in heaven give good gifts to those who ask him!"

Do you know God wants to prosper you? The truth is God first and foremost loves you and wants a personal relationship with you. But once that relationship is started, he then wants to prosper you. For those of you who are parents, don't you want to give your children good gifts? No matter how good of a parent any of us are, God is the perfect father, and he wants his children to prosper. Today, if there is an area where you have a need, ask God and watch him work. He loves to bless his sons and daughters!

THE TAKEAWAY: Money never made a man rich. Prosperity with God does not always equal money.

AUGUST 3RD

Romans 6:14—"You are not under the law, but under grace."

Wow, thank God! Before Jesus died on the cross and rose from the grave, the world was under the Old Covenant, the law. Living under law meant that everyone was to keep and fully obey the Ten Commandments and other laws of righteousness. The problem is no one is perfect, except for Jesus! However, this verse says, "You are not under law, but under grace" and grace is undeserved favor. Today, God wants to give that undeserved love to you in spite of all your mistakes. Receive God's grace today, and know that when you go to him to ask forgiveness, he will give it to you. And secondly, give that unmerited favor and love of God to others. They don't deserve it, but neither do we. God is good!

THE TAKEAWAY: A sign that someone truly understands grace is that he or she is always giving away grace to others. You can't achieve grace; you can only receive grace.

AUGUST 4TH

Romans 9:26—"They will be called children of the living God."

The greatest title in the world is not president, king, or boss. The greatest title in the world is child of God. Friend, the Lord himself could call us subjects, slaves, or workers. However, he chooses another name, son. He chooses another name, daughter. There is so much power packed into the words *son* and *daughter.* Children get the inheritance of the father. Children get the protection of the father. And children also get the name of the father. Today, reflect on this wonderful truth that you are God's child.

THE TAKEAWAY: Our identity doesn't come from us. Our identity comes from God. Know who you are in him.

AUGUST 5TH

Isaiah 55:8—"For my thoughts are not your thoughts."

We say it is impossible...God says, "Nothing is impossible."
We say I am tired...God says, "I will give you rest."
We say I can't go...God says, "My grace is sufficient."
We say I can't figure it out...God says, "I will give you wisdom."
We say I am alone...God says, "I will never leave you nor forsake you."

God is for you!

THE TAKEAWAY: Make sure your words and thoughts are lining up with God's.

AUGUST 6TH

Proverbs 18:21—"The tongue has the power of life and death."

What are you saying about yourself? Are you saying you'll never lose weight? Are you telling people you never have enough money? Have you told close friends that you are not able to do a certain task? Friend, what we say needs to line up with what God says. He says we can do all things. Life is in the tongue and so is death. Be careful how you speak and choose your words. If you constantly speak negative things over your life that is what you will receive. In order to see great things for your life, you must say great things. Agree with what God says about you.

THE TAKEAWAY: Your life will receive so much power if you will simply agree with what God says about you. In order to see great things, you must say great things!

AUGUST 7TH

Romans 14:23—"Everything that does not come from faith is sin."

Do you realize how powerful faith is? Faith sees the improbable, believes the impossible, and receives the incredible. Faith starts with nothing but ends up with everything.

Today, believe God in faith for what you need. Faith is like a muscle: the more we use it, the bigger it grows.

THE TAKEAWAY: Feed your faith, starve your doubts and don't quit.

AUGUST 8TH

Ephesians 2:14—"For he himself is our peace."

Today, millions of people are saddened by the state of their country. Friend, regardless of how our national leaders perform and regardless of who gets elected into political offices, our peace and fulfillment in life can never come from the government. Our peace and fulfillment can only come from a personal relationship with Jesus. Today, regardless if you are excited or saddened by the direction of our country, turn to the Prince of Peace for peace—Jesus!

THE TAKEAWAY: When Jesus is your peace, then your peace can never be taken away. If peace for your life is found in anyone other than Jesus, it won't last.

AUGUST 9TH

1 Corinthians 3:9—"You are God's field, God's building."

Do you know how important you are? The truth is you are more valuable than you may fully comprehend. This verse says that we are "God's field, God's building." For those whose faith is in Jesus, God truly lives in you, and you and I are his. So, if thoughts fill your mind that say you aren't important or valuable, those statements couldn't be further from the truth. You are important to God, and he has a huge plan and destiny for your life, and that truth is all that counts.

THE TAKEAWAY: An owner is the one who determines the value of the possessions owned. God values you more than you can understand!

AUGUST 10TH

Proverbs 16:3—"Commit to the Lord whatever you do, and he will establish your plans."

Is your life truly committed to God? What about your dreams and plans, are those committed to God? In order to have true success, you must commit to the Lord whatever you do. Friend, when we commit our lives and plans to God, he orders our steps and keeps our priorities straight. As you go through this day, anytime you begin to feel like you are failing in an area or just lacking, remember to commit that issue to God because he wants you to succeed. Nothing that you are facing now or in the future is too big for God!

THE TAKEAWAY: We are all committed to something. The question is, what are we committed to?

AUGUST 11TH

Proverbs 17:14—"Starting a quarrel is like breaching a dam; so drop the matter before a dispute breaks out."

Is there someone who is getting under your skin? Is there a person in your life who just knows what buttons to push and is constantly pushing them? It doesn't matter if he or she started something with you or if you started something with him or her. The key is, when someone wants to dispute and quarrel with you, the answer is not to verbally attack the person, or think of the best comeback, or slander his or her name. The answer is to drop the matter altogether. It is so easy to be angered or offended by another person. However, if we hold on to that anger or pain, the only person who gets hurt is us. Today let the love of God help you to drop "it," whatever "it" may be.

THE TAKEAWAY: The ability for a believer to flourish is directly linked to his or her ability to let go of the nagging situations that can occur in relationships.

AUGUST 12TH

1 Corinthians 9:24—"Do you not know that in a race all the runners run, but only one gets the prize? Run in such a way as to get the prize."

This day, reflect on this one thought that God wants you to win in the race of life. The end of this verse talks about getting the prize. I encourage you: in your marriage, keep running. In your job, keep running. With your son or daughter, keep running. With that situation at work, keep running. With a big dream you have for your life, keep running. Don't give up. Ask anyone who has ever won a championship if the work he or she put in was worth it. The champion will always say yes. God has not given up on you; so don't give up on yourself!

THE TAKEAWAY: The only way you are guaranteed to lose is if you quit.

AUGUST 13TH

*Colossians 1:19-20—"For God was pleased to have all his fullness dwell in him…
by making peace through his blood, shed on the cross."*

Are you having trouble sleeping? Do you sometimes feel overwhelmed?
God does something in this verse that no one else can do. God makes
peace. One of the many great qualities about God is that when there seems
to be no answer, he has the ability to create and make an answer. Today, if
you need peace in your heart, rest assured peace does not come in the form
of money, popularity, or power. Peace is only found in God. Turn to your
loving Father and let him make peace for you.

THE TAKEAWAY: You can't buy peace. You can only receive peace
from the One who bought our peace with his own blood, Jesus.

AUGUST 14TH

John 6:47—"Very truly I tell you, the one who believes has eternal life."

Wow, is it really that easy? Do you need to connect with God today? Maybe
you need to connect with him because you don't have enough money or
you are having struggles in a relationship with someone or maybe you are
in a lot of emotional pain. Friend, God wants to give you eternal life, and
he wants to breathe life into every area of your being. The key is simply
to believe in him. Today, believe God to bring life to every area of your
existence!

THE TAKEAWAY: Salvation is a free gift to you that costs Jesus
everything.

AUGUST 15TH

Ephesians 3:18—"Grasp how wide and long and high and deep is the love of Christ."

When I read today's amazing verse, I become speechless! Regardless of where you are in life, what is going on, what is changing or what is staying the same; God loves you more than you could ever truly comprehend. The love of God is so simple that it becomes complex. The love of God is so free, you can't buy it. The love of God is so valuable, you can't earn it. Just consider that you are the focus of God's love.

THE TAKEAWAY: You can never understand who you are in Christ until you consider the sacrifice Jesus made to bring you into the family.

AUGUST 16TH

1 John 1:8—"If we claim to be without sin, we deceive ourselves and the truth of God is not in us."

It is impossible to be perfect. This verse talks about those who think they have it all together. If this statement happens to describe you, then you are deceiving yourself. Friend, God knows we are not perfect. Many people kill themselves trying to be perfect. The good news is that God's Son Jesus was perfect and when we do mess up we can go to God and receive his grace. Today, have peace in the fact that God knows you are a work in progress.

THE TAKEAWAY: We might not be what we ought to be, but we aren't what we used to be either. Continue taking steps toward God and everything will work out.

AUGUST 17TH

Proverbs 21:31—"Victory rests with the Lord."

Are you walking in victory? By that, I mean are you overcoming in life or is life overwhelming you? This verse says that, "Victory rests with the Lord." Today, if you will make sure that your plans, dreams, and all of you are with the Lord, you can have his victory in any area of your life. Sometimes we find ourselves so desperate to win in life that we try to take shortcuts. Friend, there is no shortcut to having the victory of God. All of our strength has to come from him.

THE TAKEAWAY: Where have you tried to take shortcuts in life? Have you learned from those failed shortcuts? Shortcuts always lead to regrets.

AUGUST 18TH

2 Corinthians 1:3-4—"The God of all comfort, who comforts us in all our troubles, so that we can comfort those in any trouble with the comfort we ourselves receive from God."

Did you notice two powerful points in these verses? First, God can comfort us through any and all troubles we face. Secondly, we are to let him use us to comfort others. Friend, if you need comfort, don't believe the lie that what you are going through is too much or too big. Secondly, throughout today, let God use you to bring healing to other people's lives.

THE TAKEAWAY: God uses people to heal people. Who are you going to partner with God to help heal today?

AUGUST 19TH

John 8:32—"Then you will know the truth, and the truth will set you free."

Truth defined means "conformity with fact." Are you conforming to the fact today that God wants you to have limitless supernatural power in your life? Every single time we worry or doubt, we are taking our eyes off of God and putting them on ourselves. The truth breaks all chains and bondages. A believer who truly knows who he or she is in Christ can never be permanently held down. Let this truth set you free!

THE TAKEAWAY: The first step to all bondages always believes a lie from the devil. You can never be free from bondages unless you know the truth.

AUGUST 20TH

2 Corinthians 1:24—"It is by faith you stand firm."

A wise man once said, "If you don't live for something, you will fall for anything." Are you taking a stand today? Are you standing on God's promises for your life? Do you truly believe that God can and will heal, prosper, bless, guide, and give you his wisdom? Friend that is what God does. However, you have to stand firm. Just because one of God's promises for your life is delayed doesn't mean it is denied! God is for you so stand firm.

THE TAKEAWAY: It is time to stand up, not sit down. It is time to speak up, not shut up. Stand firm in the Lord!

AUGUST 21ST

Titus 3:14—"Our people must learn to devote themselves to doing what is good."

If you want to live a good life, here are three quick keys to achieving that:

1) Finish what you start.
2) Don't let your failures become final.
3) Never give up.

THE TAKEAWAY: What is it you have started that you need to finish? Identify that task and start on it again today until it is finished!

AUGUST 22ND

Romans 12:10—"Honor one another above yourselves."

This verse can be difficult to do! The Bible clearly teaches us to put others first. Friend, when we follow this instruction, we allow the love and power of God to move in our lives. Today, find ways to honor and put others ahead of yourself. For example, if you are struggling in your relationship with your spouse, chances are you might be putting your own needs first. Therefore, if you want to improve your marriage, discover ways to put your spouse's needs before your own. If you want to improve your work environment, put your coworkers first. God wants to bless your relationships. Always remember to put God first, then others, and then yourself. You will be amazed by the transformation in your relationships!

THE TAKEAWAY: Honoring someone above yourself is truly a test to see how mature your faith is in God. Are you passing the test?

AUGUST 23RD

2 Corinthians 3:17—"Now the Lord is the Spirit, and where the Spirit of the Lord is, there is freedom."

Are you free? Sometimes, the most unlikely people can be bound to an addiction. It might be dependence on drugs or alcohol. It could be an addiction to pornography, peer pressure, or depression. No matter how big or small the addiction, God wants you and me totally free. Friend, you can be free not because of what you did, but because of what Jesus has already done. You can be free not because of your willpower to say no to sin, but because Jesus said no and paid the price for our sin. Today, you can be free not because you're perfect, but because Jesus was perfect. God has unlocked your cell door, but you have to walk out.

THE TAKEAWAY: A great escape artist couldn't unlock the door to the prison cell he was placed in. Come to find out, the cell door was unlocked the entire time. This illustration is a picture of a believer who is in bondage.

AUGUST 24TH

Psalm 100:3—"Know that the Lord is God."

Basically, we all know there is a creator. But do you know there is a God? Not just a God but also a loving Father? Today, you might have head knowledge that there is a God. But if you are suffering from worry or doubt, your heart may not truly comprehend the truth about God being your Lord. No matter what you are going through, God is not overwhelmed. The Lord is God, Ruler, and King of the entire universe. Yield to his rule over every area of your life.

THE TAKEAWAY: Is there an area of your life that you are keeping from God? To be honest, you really can't keep anything from God. It is so much easier to surrender to God than to fight him. Also, it is a lot less painful.

AUGUST 25TH

Psalm 23:1—"The Lord is my shepherd, I lack nothing."

Do you know you are secure? Not because of where you live. Not because of any military, police or emergency personnel departments. Friend, we are safe because God promises to be our shepherd. Sadly, some fathers are not protectors of their own families, but God is! *Shepherd* means to guard. Today, let God not only be your loving Father but also your protecting shepherd. Trust him to protect you and he will!

THE TAKEAWAY: When a shepherd deals forcefully with the sheep, it isn't to harm them but protect them. If things are tough in your life, it might be God guiding you to safety.

AUGUST 26TH

2 Corinthians 4:18—"So we fix our eyes not on what is seen, but on what is unseen."

What are your eyes fixed on today? Are you focused on your problems? Are you focused on the negative issues that would keep you from God's very best? Friend, God wants you focused on the unseen! The unseen is God's provision for our needs; the unseen is God's favor for our lives; the unseen is the answers to our deepest needs. So, even though you might not see it, the truth is God loves you, and he is working and moving on your behalf.

THE TAKEAWAY: We can never trust what we see. We have to trust what we know.

AUGUST 27TH

2 Corinthians 6:2—*"Now is the time of God's favor, now is the day of salvation."*

Favor means a kind act, high regard, or to prefer. Friend, God wants you to have his favor for your life. If you have God's favor, no matter what the economy or newspapers report, you will be blessed. Notice the Bible uses the word *now*. Today, God wants to give you his strength, grace, and power. However, anything worth having usually requires a fight. Sometimes you have to fight for and wait to receive the very best. Don't let average become what you accept. God wants you to have his favor. Believe it and fight for it!

THE TAKEAWAY: Just because you are having trials, this doesn't mean you are out of God's will. Perhaps the trials you are facing are a confirmation you are in God's will.

AUGUST 28TH

James 4:7—*"Submit yourselves, then, to God."*

Submitting is one of the toughest things to do. At times, God will ask you to do something you don't want to do. He might ask you to do something you aren't comfortable with doing. He could even ask you to do things that are embarrassing to you. However, spiritual maturity isn't found in following our own desires. Spiritual maturity is found in submitting to God and his will. The next time you are tempted to submit to your own fleshly desires instead of submitting to God, just remember how that choice turned out for you the last time.

THE TAKEAWAY: We all submit. The question is, what are we submitting to? The most powerful men and women of God have trained themselves to submit to God quickly.

AUGUST 29TH

Psalm 3:5—"I lie down and sleep; I wake again, because the Lord sustains me."

Are you having trouble sleeping? In all of our lives there is a battle going on. The battle is over who will be in charge of our lives. Friend this is one battle you don't want to win. If you will allow God to be completely in charge of your life you can rest. God is up and he is watching over you, your family, your home, and everything. We can sleep because he sustains us. Tonight, when you lie down, lay your burdens down and enjoy the rest only God can give.

THE TAKEAWAY: We can never walk in God's rest if we have to be in control of our own lives.

AUGUST 30TH

John 17:10—"All I have is yours, and all you have is mine."

Does God's Word really say this verse? Yes! If your faith is in Jesus as your Lord and Savior, God makes an outlandish promise. You can get a glimpse of this promise in earthly homes. Fathers leave their possessions to their children in a will. God left us his provision in his will, the Bible. We need to spend time studying God's love note to us. The more we read and understand God's Word, the more power we will have to accept the promises of God.

THE TAKEAWAY: You can never accept a gift from God if your hands are already full of something else. When we position ourselves to receive from God that is when we are able to receive all that God has for us.

AUGUST 31ST

Psalm 6:9—"The Lord accepts my prayer."

This verse is great news! This one promise is what every person desires, acceptance. No matter how wealthy, how tough, or how powerful, every person desires acceptance. Friend, here is the secret. Every person has already been accepted because of God's unconditional love, but there are many who don't receive that acceptance. Listen! No matter what you have done, how you have failed, where you have sinned, God loves you and for those who receive Jesus as their Savior, you are accepted.

THE TAKEAWAY: Many times, we accept what we should refuse and we refuse what we should accept. Is there something in your life you need to refuse so you can accept what God has for you?

SEPTEBMER 1ST

Psalm 8:6—"You put everything under their feet."

God has given you authority. One time after a mission's trip I was returning back to America. There was a long line of people wanting to get into the country but they had to go through an extensive process. However, once I showed my identification I was immediately allowed to enter the United States. I was allowed in not because of any authority I had earned but because of the authority given to me by my earthly father. My father raised me in America and I was given the rights of a citizen. You are a citizen of heaven and because of that you have authority to place what you are struggling with under your feet.

THE TAKEAWAY: Many people have authority but don't use it. Are you using the authority God has given you?

SEPTEMBER 2ND

Psalm 11:1—"In the Lord I take refuge."

One time, my wife and I were in Key West, and we were riding a motor scooter, checking out the sites. All of the sudden, the skies quickly turned grey, and it started to pour down rain. We were getting soaked and we couldn't see. Finally, we got under a shelter and were able to relax. As I read this scripture, it made me think about how at times we all run around with anxiety, pain in our hearts, or futility in our lives. What is the answer that can bring genuine help? We need to get under a shelter and take refuge. Today, God wants to be that shelter, and all we have to do is take refuge under his loving arms.

THE TAKEAWAY: When the storms of life occur, who or what are you taking refuge in?

SEPTEMBERT 3RD

Psalm 12:7—"You, Lord, will keep the needy safe and will protect us forever."

Wow! This world and the people in it need to hear and believe this verse! Today, our trust must be in God for our ultimate safety. Not only in this life but also beyond. I encourage you to place your marriage, your relationships, your money goals, and your life dreams in God's hands. His protection is for you.

THE TAKEAWAY: We live in a culture where we act like money will buy everything, including safety. The safest place you can be is right where God wants you.

SEPTEMBER 4TH

Psalm 130:8—"He himself will redeem Israel from all their sins."

What do you need redeemed today? The word *redeem* can be defined as to fulfill or recover. God is in the business of recovering what we have lost. Have you lost a relationship, your temper, a business opportunity, or perhaps the respect of someone you love? Maybe you feel as though someone stole a friendship, some of your possessions, or maybe something dear to your heart. Good news! God can fulfill or recover what you feel like someone or the devil has stolen!

THE TAKEAWAY: Nothing is so lost that God can't recover it.

SEPTEMBER 5TH

Psalm 81:1—"Sing for joy to God our strength."

Happiness and joy are choices. Our circumstances don't choose our attitude. Our amount of income doesn't determine our attitude. Even our friends don't choose our attitude, we do. So, in the midst of the grind of life, the economy, and the daily issues we all face, what kind of attitude will you have? I can tell you what attitude God wants you to have, joy! You get to choose. Today, break the cycle of negativity and choose joy.

THE TAKEAWAY: What choices are you making today? Are you making choices you can only enjoy today? These are the harmful choices. Choices you can enjoy tomorrow—those are the ones you want to make.

SEPTEMBER 6TH

Psalm 13:3—"Give light to my eyes."

This could be a prayer we all need to pray. It is so hard to move around in darkness without a light. At times the world we live in can be very dark. However, God has the ability to light our way. Do you need God to turn the light on in an area of your life? He can give you the ability to see and understand no matter how painful or confusing a situation can be.

THE TAKEAWAY: Today if you feel like you're just aimlessly wandering around in life, make this verse your prayer.

SEPTEMBER 7TH

Psalm 21:11—"Though they plot evil against you and devise wicked schemes, they cannot succeed."

Today, the good news is God is for you. However, the bad news is often people, our past, our bad choices, or some other forces of evil are trying to drag us down. God gives us great news with this verse, "They cannot succeed." As you go through your day, if evil or wicked schemes come against you, remember that with God, no matter what you are facing, "they cannot succeed."

THE TAKEAWAY: Your mind-set changes when you go into a battle knowing you can't lose!

SEPTEMBER 8TH

Isaiah 38:17—"You have put all my sins behind your back."

Has a thought or idea ever just hit you? As I was reading this verse, a thought came to my mind that the only thing God turns his back on is our sins and mistakes. God promises in Joshua 1:5, "I will never leave you nor forsake you." Jesus says in Matthew 28:20, "I am with you always." The truth is God won't deny us; he won't leave us; he won't strand us on some deserted island. The good news is the only thing God will turn his back on is our mistakes. What a great and loving God we have!

THE TAKEAWAY: Don't buy into the enemy's lie that God has turned his back on you. You might be taking a test in life, but just remember back to elementary school that the teacher doesn't talk when administering the test. Don't mistake God's silence for turning his back on you. Often when you don't hear God talking, he is just letting you take the test.

SEPTEMBER 9TH

Mark 8:5—"'How many loaves do you have?' Jesus asked. 'Seven,' they replied."
Mark 8:8—"The people ate and were satisfied. Afterward the disciples picked up seven basketfuls of broken pieces that were left over."

God is a God of more than enough! Notice Jesus took seven loaves and fed over four thousand and still had leftovers. Sometimes, Christians make the mistake of just asking God for enough to scrape by in life. Friend, God doesn't want you to scrape by; he wants to give you more than enough. Today, believe him for more than enough in your dreams, job, heart, life, you name it!

THE TAKEAWAY: Pray big! Don't make the mistake of settling. God has the ability to go beyond what you could imagine.

SEPTEMBER 10TH

2 Corinthians 4:8—"We are hard pressed on every side, but not crushed."

Have you ever felt as though you were being pressed in on every side? I know I have! There have been times I was surrounded by so much stress, guilt, or pressure that I could hardly stand it. Friend, the good news is that even when we are hard pressed on every side, we won't be crushed. God does not want you to be overwhelmed by this life's burdens. Today, if you feel as though everything is caving in, remember with God, you have his promise of protection!

THE TAKEAWAY: Consider the pressure an archer creates by pulling on the bow. The further the bow is pulled back, the further the arrow can go. The same can be said of us. When God allows us to feel pressure, it is so that we are able to go further in our lives.

SEPTEMBER 11TH

Isaiah 42:16—"I will turn the darkness into light before them."

Are you in the dark today? There is darkness in pain, depression, anger, loneliness, self-esteem issues, confusion, shame, and guilt. God makes a promise that he will turn darkness into light. Notice the exact words are *I will*. God does not say, "I might," or even "I can." Friend, if there is an area of darkness in your life today, give that to God and receive his promise, "I will turn the darkness into light before them."

THE TAKEAWAY: God wants to take our pain and give us peace. When you feel like darkness is starting to overtake you, let God light your way.

SEPTEMBER 12TH

Philippians 3:13—"But one thing I do: Forgetting what is behind."

You want to talk about a difficult task? Trying to forget what is behind! That can be easier said than done at times. God has this verse in the Bible because God wants you to move past the past. Friend, is there something that is in your past that still troubles you? Perhaps a serious mistake you made? Maybe a momentary lapse in judgment? Or maybe your problem with the past is not being able to forgive someone who harmed you. Regardless of whether you hurt yourself or somebody else hurt you, let the past go! You can give your past to God, and he won't give it back.

THE TAKEAWAY: Giving our past to God requires persistence. Once you give your past to God, if the enemy starts to bring up your past, remind him of his future.

SEPTEMBER 13TH

Philippians 4:13—"I can do all this through him who gives me strength."

This next question may sound basic, but what part of the word *all* do you not understand? God gives us an incredible promise, that we can do all this through him. Anytime we try to do something great or larger than ourselves, there is always that small voice that says you can't! Friend that voice simply isn't from God. Today, dream big! Don't listen to all the reasons you can't do things; start listing the reasons you can. In your life, the only person who can limit God is you. You can do all things!

THE TAKEAWAY: In your life, you are the only person who can limit you.

SEPTEMBER 14TH

Colossians 1:12—"Giving joyful thanks to the Father, who has qualified you to share in the inheritance."

There is no way for us to be perfect and qualify for God's inheritance on our own. However, this verse gives us great excitement because the Bible says, "the Father who has qualified you." Friend, we are able to have a relationship with God because of Jesus's love and sacrifice on the cross. God says we are qualified. That means because of God's love our imperfections can be covered. Today, remember that because of Jesus you are qualified to enjoy God's salvation, strength, love, grace, peace, joy, and so much more.

THE TAKEAWAY: You are not qualified to have an amazing life because of who you are. You are qualified to have a God-filled, adventurous life because of whose you are.

SEPTEMBER 15TH

John 3:16—"For God so loved the world that he gave his one and only Son, that whoever believes in him shall not perish but have eternal life."

This one verse provides hope for the world. I want to highlight two words: *gave* and *believe*. God is a giver, and he wants to give you his strength, power, and wisdom today. God also wants you to believe. We need to believe in what might seem impossible to our minds. Once we start believing, it is then we can start receiving.

THE TAKEAWAY: Consider this, you are never more like God than when you give.

SEPTEMBER 16TH

Isaiah 45:21—"Declare what is to be."

Friend, this verse is a powerful principle. What happens when you say you are going to fail? You fail. What happens when you say you can't do it? You can't do it. Today, God wants us to declare what is to be. So, when it seems like your family is falling apart declare that your family is whole and is growing closer every day. Maybe you are struggling with money; declare that things are turning around in your favor. It easy to declare good things when things are going well. It takes spiritual character and tenacity to declare God's blessings in the face of trials. Declare God's blessings for your life!

THE TAKEAWAY: Boldly declare the blessings of God over every area of your life and don't stop!

SEPTEMBER 17TH

Colossians 3:15—"And be thankful."

There is a lot of turmoil in our world today. We don't have to look far to see someone who is hurting or just barely getting by in life. Maybe you are the one who feels discouraged today. I want to encourage you to still be thankful. You might say, "You don't know what I am facing," and this is true. However, God knows and he says, "Be thankful." Friend, when we are thankful, we get our eyes focused on what is important in life. Secondly, when our hearts are thankful, we position ourselves to be blessed by God. When we are truly thankful, we are then able to receive God's power to turn around any situation we are facing.

THE TAKEAWAY: When we aren't thankful, we are the ones keeping God's power out of our lives.

SEPTEMBER 18TH

Romans 8:35—"Who shall separate us from the love of Christ?"

Do you feel God's love for you today? If you don't, it isn't because God doesn't love you. No, it is the opposite. God loves you, and there is nothing you can do to stop it. He has a relentless love toward you and me. That is such good news! Today we need to turn to God, but even if you don't, he still loves you and always will. What a wonderful and loving God he is.

THE TAKEAWAY: The devil can never defeat you as long as you know and agree with what God's Word says about you.

SEPTEMBER 19TH

Psalm 32:7—"You will protect me from trouble."

What trouble are you facing today? What is causing stress in your life? Are you trying to fight and face it yourself or are you asking God to protect you? If you want to wear yourself out, try to do what only God can do. Friend, God's desire is to protect you. As you face the daily grind of life, don't forget that you can run to God and he will protect you from trouble.

THE TAKE WAY: When you do your part, which is running to God, he will do his part of protecting you.

SEPTEMBER 20TH

Psalm 32:5—"And you forgave the guilt of my sin."

Do you feel guilty today or have you struggled with guilt in the past? Friend, not only does God want to forgive your sin but he wants to remove the guilt as well! Initially, having remorse for sins you have committed is a good sign that you are listening to God to repent. But once you ask God to forgive you, he does, and as a result, you are no longer guilty, you are free. Today, you can have peace in knowing that God not only forgives us, but he removes our guilt from the poor choices we have made. He loves us that much!

THE TAKEAWAY: The strength of sin is in secrecy. When you expose sin to the light of God, its power is removed.

SEPTEMBER 21ST

1 Corinthians 13:4—"Love is patient"

Patience is not one of my strengths. However, when it comes to family, friends, and relationships, patience is a must. One indication we truly love someone is when we show that person patience. No doubt being patient is easier said than done. But we must remember that God is always patient with us in so many ways we simply don't deserve. When you are tempted to be impatient with someone you love, remember how patient God is with you and do likewise.

THE TAKEAWAY: Patience is a test of love. Make sure you pass this test when you deal with those you love in your life.

SEPTEMBER 22ND

1 Thessalonians 2:13—"The word of God, which is indeed at work in you who believe."

Friend, today God wants to work in your life. God wants to bless you. However, the key is we must believe. Today, believe God to work on your behalf. Believe him for that promotion or family situation to be resolved. Believe God to open up opportunities, or to bring healing to your heart, or to help you get your finances in order. Basically, if you don't believe, the chances are you may never receive.

THE TAKEAWAY: We make choices and God makes changes. When you make godly choices, you will start to see godly changes in your life!

SEPTEMBER 23RD

Romans 10:12—"The same Lord is Lord of all and richly blesses all who call on him."

God loves you and he loves everyone in this world! There is nothing we can or can't do to change God's unconditional love for us. However, notice two details about this verse. First, not only does God want to bless you, he wants to *"richly"* bless you. The word *rich* is often defined as abundant, so God wants to abundantly bless you. Secondly, notice this abundant blessing comes to those who *"call on him."* Friend, have you called on God today? God will abundantly bless you when you call on him to be Lord of your life.

THE TAKEAWAY: You can't ask little and receive large. If you ask little, you will receive little. But if you ask large, then you will receive large.

SEPTEMBER 24TH

Psalm 34:4—"He delivered me from all my fears."

What are you afraid of? Are you fearful of losing your job, making a mistake, losing a relationship, or maybe being alone? Are you scared that you might not get another chance, that you have lost a friend, or that maybe you will never find your future spouse? Whatever you are afraid or scared of, remember that God wants to deliver you from all your fears. If you are a believer in Jesus, you can say goodbye to your fears.

THE TAKEAWAY: You can't remove a fearful thought or really any thought at all. But you can replace a thought. Identify the thoughts that need to be removed from your life and replace those with God's Word.

SEPTEMBER 25TH

Isaiah 52:12—"The God of Israel will be your rear guard."

You may have heard the saying, "I've got your back." This is a popular phrase we say to people to let them know we are watching out for them. However, we can't physically be with and protect the people we love all the time. I pray for God to protect my wife; however, when we wake up and both go to work, in our hearts we don't leave each other, but in reality, we are apart. The good news is God makes this huge claim that he will protect and guard us even from behind. Today, I want to encourage you "God has your back." You can trust him!

THE TAKEAWAY: You can't trust both God and yourself. Somebody has to be in charge of your life. Either you will be in charge and put your trust in man, or God will be in charge of your life and you will put your trust in God.

SEPTEMBER 26TH

Psalm 46:10—"Be still, and know that I am God."

Do you need to turn down the volume of your hectic life? Sometimes our job, our families, or our plans can make life so demanding and loud we can't enjoy it. Today, God wants you to slow down and quiet yourself before him. Take time and try to be still today! Slow down and listen. God loves you and he wants to provide for your every need. What is so important about being still before God? We get better understanding, we get rest, and best of all, we begin to realize that God is God and he is in control. Therefore, give yourself a break, slow down and take time to listen to God.

THE TAKEAWAY: One of the greatest ways to slow down is having a one-day or half-day fast from any of the distractions in your life, especially getting unplugged from the Internet or other electronics.

SEPTEMBER 27TH

Isaiah 54:17—"No weapon forged against you will prevail."

God gives us a great promise! The promise is not that weapons won't be formed against us. The promise is that those weapons will not prevail. As you go through today, you might encounter the weapon of stress, discouragement, backstabbing, fear, doubt, or you name it. However, God says, "No weapon forged against you will prevail." What God says goes. Walk in his power today and know that there might be battles, but God will not be defeated!

THE TAKEAWAY: The only way a believer can be defeated is if he or she doesn't call on the name of the Lord.

SEPTEMBER 28TH

Isaiah 55:9—"As the heavens are higher than the earth, so are my ways higher than your ways and my thoughts than your thoughts."

Have you ever tried to understand why God allowed someone to die? Do you wonder sometimes why some people have very little and other people have too much? Perhaps you tried to figure out why God has you in the situation you are currently facing. Friend, you won't be able to figure out or understand God completely! If we could fully comprehend God, he wouldn't be God. This verse says his ways and thoughts are higher than ours. Today, I want to encourage you to grasp the concept that God is for you and not against you. You will wear yourself out trying to understand everything about how God works. Know that he is in control and he has a great plan for your life!

THE TAKEAWAY: If we could fully understand God, he wouldn't be God.

SEPTEMBER 29TH

John 3:16—"For God so loved the world."

There is nothing you will face today that will surprise God. In our lives:

* We say nobody loves me, but God says I love you.
* We say I'm always worried and frustrated, and God says cast all your cares upon me.
* We say I feel alone, and God says I will never leave you nor forsake you.
* We say I can't manage, and God says I will supply all your needs.
* We say I am tired, and God says I will give you rest.

Isn't God good?

THE TAKEAWAY: If we let our feelings lead us, we will always be defeated. True power unfolds in our lives when we trust what we know to be true in God's Word, not what we feel.

SEPTEMBER 30TH

Psalm 37:4—"Take delight in the Lord, and he will give you the desires of your heart."

Do you really understand God's heart toward you? Friend, God wants to give you the desires of your heart. Many times, people misunderstand God and think that following him prohibits them from certain freedoms or pleasures. The opposite is true! Following God unlocks certain pleasures and gives total freedom. God yearns for us to delight in him and he yearns to give us the desires of our hearts. It's true! Today, delight yourself in the Lord and let him bless you!

THE TAKEAWAY: Whatever thoughts dominate your mind oftentimes reveals what is most important to you. Without delighting in the Lord our desires will never be met.

OCTOBER 1ST

Isaiah 58:11—"The Lord will guide you always; he will satisfy your needs in a sun-scorched land."

Have you ever felt as if you were in a dry season in life? Have you ever had a desert experience in your job, marriage, or calling? God gives us two great promises. First, he promises to "guide you always." Secondly, he promises he will "satisfy your needs." Today, in the wilderness of life, take a moment and ask God to give you his guidance. He is always ready to give us direction, but we don't always listen and receive. Remember, he will bring the refreshing rains to end your drought by satisfying and meeting all your needs.

THE TAKEAWAY: God has amazing plans and a destiny for our lives. Trust God to guide you out of the desert and satisfy your every need.

OCTOBER 2ND

Psalm 40:2 —"He lifted me out of the slimy pit, out of the mud and mire."

God wants you out of the pit! Yes, God wants you out of the mud and mire of anger, worry, fear, loneliness, depression, guilt, shame, and the doldrums of life. The Word says, "He lifted me out of the slimy pit." Today, you might find yourself in one of the many possible slimy pits of life. Perhaps you have tried without success to get yourself out. Friend, only God can get us out of those pits! Feed your faith, doubt your doubts, and trust God to be the one who lifts you up.

THE TAKEAWAY: God doesn't just lift us out of a pit in life to only be free. God lifts us out so we can start lifting others out of their pits as well.

OCTOBER 3RD

Isaiah 64:8—"Yet you, Lord, are our father."

How is your relationship with your earthly father? Some people have amazing and some have miserable relationships with their dads. Maybe your dad treated you like gold or perhaps your dad was never there for you. Friend, God wants you to know that not only does he want to be your Lord; he also wants to be your loving Father. Today, if you have a good earthly father, honor him! If you have a distant, unloving earthly father, forgive him! Either way let God be the perfect and all loving Father to you.

THE TAKEAWAY: If your earthly father has harmed you, forgive him. Even if he hasn't asked for forgiveness, forgive him. If you don't, you are putting yourself in your own prison cell.

OCTOBER 4TH

Psalm 43:5—"Put your hope in God."

What is your hope in today? Is your hope in the government, a friend, money, or worldly possessions? Friend, we can only enjoy life when our hope is in God. This world is passing away and will never be perfect. But when our hope is in God, he is perfect and so is his plan for our lives. This day, I encourage you to put your hope in God. Once your hope is in God, you can get your hopes up for your life because he has supernatural answers for everything you may face.

THE TAKEAWAY: God has a view of our lives we simply don't have. We can trust him and put our hope in him because he sees every detail of our lives.

OCTOBER 5TH

2 Timothy 1:7—"For the Spirit God gave us does not make us timid, but gives us power, love and self-discipline."

God does not give us a spirit of fear, hate, worry, or anxiety. No, instead he gives us a spirit of power, love, and a sound mind. If you are struggling with the fear of tomorrow, anxiety about your job, or maybe you can't sleep because of worry, don't give up. Get rid of stinking thinking and receive the power, love, and sound mind God wants you to have.

THE TAKEAWAY: What bad thoughts do you need to starve? What healthy thoughts do you need to feed?

OCTOBER 6TH

Philippians 4:13—"I can do all this through him who gives me strength."

You are more powerful than you think you are. You don't have power because I say you have power. You are powerful because God gives you strength. Too many times we sell ourselves short because of our own limitations. However, you don't have limitations when your life is filled with the power and strength of Jesus. It is worth repeating the statement that you are more powerful than you think you are.

THE TAKEAWAY: We can only have lives without limitations if God is the source of our power.

OCTOBER 7TH

Proverbs 3:5-6—"Trust in the Lord with all your heart and lean not on your own understanding; in all your ways submit to him, and he will make your paths straight."

Why should we trust in the Lord? Here are some thoughts to consider:

1) God loves us more than we could ever fathom.
2) He promises never to forsake us even when we have made mistakes.
3) He knows the past, present and future.
4) He wants the very best for our lives.
5) He has great plans for each of us.
6) He is good and all knowing.
7) He accepts us unconditionally.
8) He longs to have a loving personal relationship with each of us.

Trust him today and he will make your paths straight.

THE TAKEAWAY: Nobody dies and goes to heaven thinking he or she trusted God too much. No, when we die, many of us will look back on our lives wishing we had trusted God more.

OCTOBER 8TH

1 Corinthians 15:57—"But thanks be to God! He gives us the victory through our Lord Jesus Christ."

Did you know there are a few things God has never seen? God has never seen a situation he couldn't turn around, a heart he couldn't heal, a life he couldn't change, a sin he couldn't forgive, a life he doesn't love, and a person he couldn't use. Today, start viewing God through the light of his power to do more than you could ask or imagine.

THE TAKEAWAY: Ask God to help you see every area of your life through his eyes. Also, ask God to help you perceive yourself through his eyes. You are a victor!

OCTOBER 9TH

1 Timothy 6:12—"Fight the good fight of the faith."

Today, what are you fighting for? Many times, the things we value in life will require a fight. For me, I had to fight to lose fifty pounds and keep it off to have good health. For some, it might be a fight to graduate from high school or college. For those in a marriage, you might fight to keep the relationship with your spouse healthy. Today, I want to encourage you to fight for your dreams and fight for your goals! Let me encourage you to believe God and fight for what you might think is impossible! God is for you!

THE TAKEAWAY: Anything worth having is worth fighting for.

OCTOBER 10TH

Psalm 48:14—"He will be our guide even to the end."

I am going to ask you to do something that may be difficult to do. Before you make any decisions today, set aside at least five minutes to ask God to guide you. I am serious. This five-minute plan will bless you and will make a positive difference in the choices you make. There is power when we seek God and ask him for his guidance. Friend, you deserve God's very best, but sometimes our own choices keep us from his very best. Take the five-minute challenge today and let God guide your steps.

THE TAKEAWAY: When we yield to God, he will be the one in charge of our life and will give us trustworthy guidance.

OCTOBER 11TH

Titus 3:5—"He saved us, not because of righteous things we had done, but because of his mercy."

Do you need some grace today? There is a popular acronym that helps explain what grace means: G=God's R=Riches A=At C=Christ's E=Expense! When you make a mistake in life, there is grace. If you have let someone down, there is grace. The trick of the devil is to get you focused on your own mistakes and failures. We need God's grace to move past our mistakes and then not to repeat them. God gives us what we don't deserve because of the amazing sacrifice of Jesus. Today, receive the riches and blessings of God through his grace.

THE TAKEAWAY: Out of our brokenness, God brings blessing.

OCTOBER 12TH

Ephesians 3:20—"Now to him who is able to do immeasurably more."

Do you know God can do more in your life than can even be measured? The word *measured* means determining the extent, dimensions or quantity of something. God is so loving, and his power so beyond our comprehension, that we can't even begin to measure it. Today, if you feel as though you are encountering an impossible situation or you are facing a giant, just remember God's power is so substantial it can't be measured.

THE TAKEAWAY: The devil and his attacks on your life have limits. God and his power for your life have no limits.

OCTOBER 13TH

Psalm 108:12—"Give us aid against the enemy, for human help is worthless."

Have you ever faced a problem with the wrong answer? Perhaps you have had a square peg for a round hole? Many times, we face issues or problems, but we don't have the right answer to our problem. In life, some problems can't be fixed by a friend or family member. Most of life's deepest aches and pains can only be healed by God. Today, as you go through life, understand a human being can't fix your every problem. God can do in one second what no person can do in a hundred years. Let God be the one to give you aid today.

THE TAKEAWAY: God wants to give us help and answers to our issues. However, the problem is not in God wanting to give us help. Oftentimes, the problem is in us receiving help from God.

OCTOBER 14TH

Matthew 18:21-22—"Lord, how many times shall I forgive my brother or sister who sins against me? Up to seven times? Jesus answered, 'I tell you, not seven times, but seventy-seven times.'"

Do you need a second chance in some area of your life? Do you need a redo? Good news, this verse is a picture of God's forgiveness and the ability for all of us to get a new start. I love the phrase, "fresh start." Where do you need one today? Jesus was asked if forgiveness should be given up to seven times, and his reply was not seven times, but seventy-seven times. If you are trying to calculate that in your mind, you have missed it. The point is God's grace is extensive. Today, if you need a fresh start in any area of your life, turn to God, believe and receive it!

THE TAKEAWAY: If you want to receive God's forgiveness, you have to forgive others. Not forgiving someone is like drinking poison and expecting it to hurt him or her.

OCTOBER 15TH

Psalm 53:5—"But there they are, overwhelmed with dread, where there was nothing to dread."

Have you ever wasted time worrying about something you later found out you had no reason for worrying? Here, this verse reveals the anxiety we experience when we worry. Today, you might be fretting over some issues in your life. Notice the above verse says. "There they are, overwhelmed with dread, where there was nothing to dread." Don't let this statement describe you. What might be bothering you today is actually small compared to God's power. The next time you find yourself being overwhelmed or worried, remember that with God you are never without hope.

THE TAKEAWAY: Think about times in your life where you worried about something you had no need to worry. Worrying is one of the all-time greatest ways to waste our lives and our time.

OCTOBER 16TH

Hebrews 4:16—"Let us then approach God's throne of grace with confidence."

I once had a great boss who said to me and everyone working for him that his door was always open to us if we ever needed anything. Guess what? God has this same open-door policy with us. As today's verse reminds us, "Let us then approach God's throne of grace with confidence." Notice God wants us to understand that we can go to him about any need we have and he will give us his grace. Friend, never forget that God's door is always open to you. We need to make a habit of walking with confidence through the threshold of his grace!

THE TAKEAWAY: There are no limits on the man or woman who has met alone with God.

OCTOBER 17TH

Psalm 124:8—"Our help is in the name of the Lord, the Maker of heaven and earth."

A name is something powerful. A name can open doors that seem to be shut down. Oftentimes, people will drop names to try and get favor or advancement. I want to encourage you that God wants you to drop and use his name. When you are in trouble, use his name. When you are filled with sorrow, use his name. When you are overcome with worry, use his name. Remember, "Our help is in the name of the Lord."

THE TAKEAWAY: Whose name are you using to accomplish your goals and visions in life? Are you using God's name or your own?

OCTOBER 18TH

Psalm 59:9—"You are my strength, I watch for you."

What are you watching for today? Are you only noticing the problems in your life or do you see the blessings? Do you only perceive the trials or can you spot the triumphs? Today, I want to encourage you to watch for God. He is moving and working on your behalf right now as you read this, but the question is are you paying attention? God is watching out for us; we need to make sure we are watching out for him. The next time you find yourself in a difficult situation, don't just focus on the problem; look at the answer. Watch for God and see how he will provide for you!

THE TAKEAWAY: It is easy to get our eyes off of God and off of what is important. Ask God to help you view your life through his point of view.

OCTOBER 19TH

Psalm 60:12—"With God we will gain the victory."

Don't we all desire to have victory in life? *Victory* defined is success or triumph in any battle or contest. We all face battles and contests throughout our lives, but God wants you to triumph! The key to victory is that two-word phrase at the beginning of this verse, "With God." If you manage your business "with God," you will succeed. If you work hard at your job "with God," you will win. If your marriage is partnered "with God," you will have victory. Today, make it your goal to do all you do "with God."

THE TAKEAWAY: Your life can be filled with victories or defeat. The choice is up to you.

OCTOBER 20TH

Psalm 61:2—"Lead me to the rock that is higher than I."

We all need stability in this unstable world. We can't rely on anything or anyone to be perfect other than Jesus. I love my wife, but neither she nor I are faultless. You love your family, but they aren't perfect either. If we build our lives on the shifting sand of this world, our plans and dreams will be shaky at best if not totally destroyed. However, if we allow our lives to be led to the solid rock of Christ, then our lives will be blessed because we have built them on a firm foundation. There is an old hymn called "My Hope is Built on Nothing Less" that has this verse, "On Christ, the solid Rock I stand; all other ground is sinking sand." Today put your trust in Jesus, the only one who is stable and unchanging.

THE TAKEAWAY: If we build our lives on anything other than the Rock, Jesus, we will find ourselves sinking in the sand.

OCTOBER 21ST

Psalm 62:8—"Pour out your hearts to him, for God is our refuge."

Have you ever had people ask you to stop complaining or to quit telling them all your problems? God is good for numerous reasons but one of the many is he desires to listen to our hearts when we have problems. Friend, we can go to God and honestly share with him all our hopes, fears, sins, struggles, and lay all those concerns at his feet. The good news is that God doesn't stop at only listening to our requests. When we pour out our hearts to him, he will actually do something about the trials we are facing! Isn't that good news?

THE TAKEAWAY: Out of our brokenness God brings blessing.

OCTOBER 22ND

Psalm 62:11—"Two things I have heard: 'Power belongs to you, God, and with you, Lord, is unfailing love.'"

You can take it to the bank: God is loving and strong. The word *strong* means vigorous, powerful, and able. No matter what issues you may be facing in your life today, know that God is vigorous, powerful, and able to help you overcome any obstacle. Take a load off today and rest in the fact that God's love and power are gifts he wants to give to you.

THE TAKEAWAY: Christ's power is made manifest only in our weakness.

OCTOBER 23RD

Psalm 63:5—"I will be fully satisfied."

Are you satisfied today? Are you content? When we try to obtain satisfaction and contentment through means other than a relationship with God, our lives will begin to feel incomplete and empty. Friend, God wants you to be fully satisfied in him. He desires to give you his love, peace, wisdom, direction, strength, and favor. Today, I encourage you to let his goodness and grace direct and fulfill your life. He wants you satisfied with his good things!

THE TAKEAWAY: We can never be fully satisfied with the things of this world. We can only find true satisfaction in our relationship with God.

OCTOBER 24TH

Hebrews 11:6—"He rewards those who earnestly seek him."

Friend, God wants to reward you! Have you ever thought about God giving you a reward? Do you know why? Over two thousand years ago, God gave his Son Jesus because he was earnestly seeking to have a personal relationship with us. When we start seeking God, we are doing to him what he has been doing to us for as long as we have been alive! Today, let God reward you; start seeking him!

THE TAKEAWAY: When we seek God, we demonstrate that we love him in return. There is no greater reward than being in God's presence.

OCTOBER 25TH

Hebrews 11:34—"Whose weakness was turned to strength."

What are your weaknesses? Where do you find yourself lacking? Friend, God can turn those weaknesses into strengths! Do you have a temper? Do you sometimes speak when you should listen? Do you spend too much money? Are you impatient? God is all-powerful and can step into any situation of your life and make changes. He wants to turn your weaknesses into strengths. Today, I challenge you to surrender those weaknesses to God. Give him the areas of your life that you feel are weak and watch him turn those areas into strong points!

THE TAKEAWAY: One of the amazing characteristics of God is that he has the ability to make the weak strong. You are stronger than you think you are!

OCTOBER 26TH

Hebrews 11:33—"Who through faith conquered kingdoms."

God wants you to be a conqueror! Are you conquering or are you getting defeated? Is there an addiction you need to conquer or maybe a fear? Today, the way we conquer issues in life is to have faith in God. Not faith in faith or faith in ourselves but faith in God. With God's help, you can conquer any obstacle you face. With God, you can overcome any setback. Today, God will help you triumph over what is holding you back in life!

THE TAKEAWAY: You can tear down strongholds. You can overcome barriers. But you just can't give up!

OCTOBER 27TH

Ephesians 4:24—"Put on the new self."

Do you need some new clothing? No, I don't mean clothing you get from the mall. I mean do you need a new attitude? Do you need a new beginning in a relationship? Do you need a new outlook? Do you need a new start where you try something different? Friend, we can enjoy life because when we put our faith and trust in the Lord we are able to "put on the new self." Today, take the fresh start God gives to you and put it on!

THE TAKEAWAY: God is more concerned with where you are going than with where you have been.

OCTOBER 28TH

Psalm 66:12—"You brought us to a place of abundance."

Do you know God wants to bring you to a place of abundance? He wants your family, marriage, emotional life, and thought life to have his abundance. *Abundance* means plentiful supply. God has a plentiful supply of love, wisdom, mercy, grace, and provision he wants to give you today. He is a good God and he wants to give to you from his overflowing supply. Do you get the point? God loves you greatly!

THE TAKEAWAY: God doesn't want you to survive in this life. God wants you to thrive!

OCTOBER 29TH

Psalm 84:7—"They go from strength to strength."

Do you feel as though sometimes you are on a roller coaster in life, up one day, down the next? God doesn't want you to go from the depths to the peaks of life and then back to the depths again. No, God wants to take you from strength to strength. God wants to give you his power, but that doesn't mean you won't ever have problems to face. It simply means you can overcome the difficulties and continue on in the joy of the Lord!

THE TAKEAWAY: Get off the roller coaster of feelings and get on to the solid rock of God's Word.

OCTOBER 30TH

1 John 5:3—"And his commands are not burdensome."

Have you ever thought that the commands of God are burdensome? Don't believe this lie! His commands are not burdens but blessings. Anytime God gives us a command, it is rooted in his desire to protect us. When God guides and directs us in our every day lives what seems to be a burden, later in life will show itself to be a blessing.

THE TAKEAWAY: A wrong thought will lead to a wrong action. A wrong action will lead to a wrong habit. A wrong habit will lead to wrong character. A wrong character will lead to a destroyed life. Make sure your thoughts line up with God's commands.

OCTOBER 31ST

Jeremiah 32:41—"I will rejoice in doing them good."

Wow, did you notice the great news in today's verse? Not only does God do good to his children but also he rejoices in it. Catch that again: he is excited to do us good. This verse along with many other verses throughout the Bible teach and demonstrate how good God is to us, and how madly in love he is with his creation. Today, as you go through life, hide in your heart the truth that God loves you and rejoices in doing good to you.

THE TAKEAWAY: God is good. We will draw closer to God when we understand that how God relates to us is based on his goodness and love for us.

NOVEMBER 1ST

John 14:27—"Do not let your hearts be troubled and do not be afraid."

There are two points to really key in on here in this part of the verse. First, the devil – he cannot make our hearts be troubled unless we let it happen. You have the power of God to resist the lies and attacks of the devil. Secondly, once we resist the devil, the Word says we don't need to be afraid. Friend, in these troubling times we face today, let the peace of God dwell in your hearts. You do not have to be filled with worry, fear or doubt. God is with you!

THE TAKEAWAY: Joy and peace are a choice.

NOVEMBER 2ND

Jeremiah 31:25—"I will refresh the weary and satisfy the faint."

Are you weary today? Not satisfied with your life, job, or a relationship? There is a key to finding refreshment and satisfaction: honestly turning to God as your complete source of life. Notice the verse says, "I will refresh." God is the one who refreshes us when we are tired and exhausted. No getaway can give you rest like meeting with God. No earthly reward can satisfy your soul like God. Truly connect with God today, and let him refresh and satisfy you.

THE TAKEAWAY: Spending time alone with God will bring refreshment to your tired and weary soul. Make sure to set aside time today to meet with God.

NOVEMBER 3RD

Jeremiah 32:27—"I am the Lord, the God of all mankind. Is anything too hard for me?"

I believe the Lord would like to ask us this question today. Is there anything in your life you think is too hard for God? Do you think that a relationship is too damaged, a job is too far out of reach, a sin too immoral to forgive, or a hurt too deep to heal? Friend, the answer to this question is NO, nothing is too hard for God! All miracles and life changes start with the one belief that nothing is impossible for God.

THE TAKEAWAY: The hardest part of receiving a miracle is taking the first steps of faith. Step out in faith and believe God for the impossible today!

NOVEMBER 4TH

Romans 8:28—"And we know that in all things God works for the good of those who love him."

Have you ever had something bad happen to you? What about something hurtful? God gives a promise that he will use all things that happen in our lives for good. Today, I want to challenge you not to perceive your hardships through the lens of "poor old me." Instead, view those adversities from the perspective of having the opportunity to experience firsthand the miracle-working power of God in your life. God will work those things out for your good.

THE TAKEAWAY: Rarely will we understand the purpose behind our pain immediately. However, if we continue to walk down the road with God, we will be able to look back and see his divine hand making those messes into a masterpiece.

NOVEMBER 5TH

2 Samuel 22:31—"The Lord's word is flawless."

Do you need some good news today? Just turn to the Bible and meditate on God's promises. The Word of God is a love letter to us reminding us that we are forgiven, healed, loved, empowered, more than conquerors, adopted into the family of God, saved, and given grace. Most of what we receive from our culture is in the form of bad news. Isn't it time to read God's Word and receive some good news?

THE TAKEAWAY: God is never nervous when you fact-check his statements. You can take God's Word to the bank; it is perfect and flawless.

NOVEMBER 6TH

Romans 5:5—"God's love has been poured out into our hearts."

God wants you to know that he has poured out his love on you. His love flows to and for you! Friend, I want to encourage you today to let that same love God has poured into your heart to flow into your relationships with your spouse, child, parent, or coworker—whoever is in your sphere of influence. Receive God's love and then share it with others.

THE TAKEAWAY: Whenever you are full of God's love, you can't help but want to give that love to others.

NOVEMBER 7TH

Philippians 4:6—"Do not be anxious about anything."

This verse can be so difficult to follow! Anxiety and worry have one thing in common: they are a complete waste of our time. We have the head knowledge that we shouldn't be anxious, but how do we really overcome anxiety in practice? One of the greatest weapons to fight anxiety is worship. Anxiety finds its root in not resting in God. Worship, on the other hand, is based on resting and trusting that God is our ultimate provider. When we spend time in the presence of God worshipping him, worry and anxiety will begin to dissipate!

THE TAKEAWAY: If you are struggling with anxiety, spend time worshipping God. Start by lifting your hands and your voice to worship the Creator of the universe!

NOVEMBER 8TH

John 8:36—"So if the Son sets you free, you will be free indeed."

Have you ever felt bound to sin, guilt, an addiction, or anything else? Friend, the Bible says Jesus came to set the captives free. Today, God wants you to know you are free. No matter what the issues are that make you feel imprisoned, God is a God who will give you freedom. Today, if you are struggling to be free in some area of your life, search for Bible verses to memorize and stand on when those issues arise. Remember that when Jesus sets you free, you are free indeed!

THE TAKEAWAY: All sin leads to captivity. The devil wants nothing more than for the saved people of God to be in bondage. However, God's will is for you to be free!

NOVEMBER 9TH

Ephesians 1:4—"For he chose us in him before the creation of the world."

You are chosen by God! Yes, God handpicked you because he wants to pour out his grace and love on you and have a living relationship with you. As you go through the day, meditate on this wonderful truth that God chose you. Even when times get tough or when you face heartache, the truth still remains that you are chosen by God and you are valuable in his eyes!

THE TAKEAWAY: The enemy can never have his plans advance in our lives if we are confident of who we are in Jesus Christ!

NOVEMBER 10TH

Mark 6:31—"Come with me by yourselves to a quiet place and get some rest."

Amen! This scripture speaks to me. Have you ever been so stressed you couldn't think or so overwhelmed you didn't know what to do? Jesus has the cure! Spend time alone with him in a quiet place and get some rest. Do you know the only place to find rest is in God? Today, I encourage you to take a retreat into the presence of God. Meet with Jesus alone and receive his rest.

THE TAKEAWAY: No degree, training, or conference can equip you for the trials of life like meeting alone with our loving Savior, Jesus.

NOVEMBER 11TH

Mark 6:56—"They begged him to let them touch even the edge of his cloak, and all who touched it were healed."

Do you need an area of your life healed today? Maybe you have a broken relationship, heartache, or a physical pain in your body? The answer is simply to touch Jesus. How do we do that? By transferring our faith in a religion and placing our trust in our miracle-working Savior! Despite any pain you might be facing, when you say, "Jesus, I put my faith in you to heal," you are acquiring supernatural power. Whether you know it or not, when you put your faith in Jesus, the gates of hell shake. What a great God we serve.

THE TAKEAWAY: Religion is man's effort to get to God. The cross of Jesus is God's effort to get to man! God wants a personal life-giving relationship with you.

NOVEMBER 12TH

Psalm 75:7—"It is God who judges."

When have you done something you weren't supposed to do? As believers in Jesus, we aren't supposed to judge other people. God has given us a new name and a new nature. Believers are not supposed to judge those around them; believers are supposed to love them instead. God is the only one who is perfect, and he is the judge. Anytime we try to do something only God is supposed to do, we are going to hurt others and strain our own relationship with God.

THE TAKEAWAY: One of the greatest tests to our godliness is examining whether or not we judge other people. The closer we get to God, the less we will judge others.

NOVEMBER 13TH

Psalm 90:12—"Teach us to number our days, that we may gain a heart of wisdom."

We all need wisdom with how to better spend our time. Could I encourage you not to put the right energy into the wrong area? Let me say that one more time. Don't put the right energy into the wrong area. We all need God's wisdom how to spend our time. Before you start investing serious amounts of time into something or someone, make sure you are investing your most precious asset in line with the will of God.

THE TAKEAWAY: You only get so many days in this life; make them count!

NOVEMBER 14TH

Mark 8:8—"The people ate and were satisfied."

Satisfied is a word few in this world really understand. Not being satisfied is why millions are in debt, millions are on drugs, and millions of marriages have been destroyed. Today, God wants you to be fulfilled and content. Trust me, the new job, the new relationship, or the next raise in pay won't ever bring genuine satisfaction. True contentment can only be found when we are walking and resting with God.

THE TAKEAWAY: Anything made by man will always leave you wanting more.

NOVEMBER 15TH

Philippians 1:2—"Grace and peace to you from God our Father and the Lord Jesus Christ."

Sometimes everything can seem to be going great outwardly in your life, but that doesn't mean inwardly you have peace. Sometimes, on the surface you can pretend that everything is fine, but on the inside you can't sleep, think, or live because you don't have peace and quiet in your soul. Friend, God wants you to have his peace. The key in this verse is to understand that grace and peace only come from God alone. Today, spend time in God's presence and receive his priceless gift of grace and peace.

THE TAKEAWAY: You can't have peace without grace.

NOVEMBER 16TH

Mark 10:15—"Truly I tell you, anyone who will not receive the kingdom of God like a little child will never enter it."

Do you have trouble trusting God at times? Every so often, I want to understand all the details of how God is going to work everything out in my life. The fact remains that we just need to trust him like children trust their parents. Today, I want to encourage you to step out and believe God to heal a relationship, provide money, give new hope, mend a broken heart, forgive a hidden sin, and so much more. God is so good; we can't even begin to fully understand it.

THE TAKEAWAY: Is your faith becoming more mature? A sign that faith is becoming more mature is that it is becoming more childlike.

NOVEMBER 17TH

Colossians 3:15—"And be thankful."

At this time of year, millions are preparing to celebrate the holiday of Thanksgiving. However, many people will miss the point of why they are celebrating in the first place. During this time, many will act thankful. They will eat a ton, watch some football, and maybe share some thankful thoughts with their families and friends. However, this verse from Colossians doesn't say act thankful, it says, "be thankful." When you are truly thankful, it is more than an act; it is a lifestyle. Be thankful for your family, friends, health, country, and the Lord not just on Thanksgiving Day but every day! Spend time today and each day being thankful you are alive, thankful for what you have, and thankful that God loves you.

THE TAKEAWAY: God's desire is that every day would be Thanksgiving in our lives!

NOVEMBRER 18TH

Romans 8:31—"If God is for us, who can be against us?"

Do you know what it means that God is for you? When I was a child, I was in a sports tournament and everybody was cheering for the boy I was up against…except my mom. She was yelling for me at the top of her lungs. She was the only one in the crowd rooting for me, but she wasn't bashful. Friend, just like my mom was there for me, God is always in your corner and is cheering you on. It doesn't matter who or what might be against you, when God is for you, he is the only one you need to be for you.

THE TAKEAWAY: If God is for you, that is all you need for your dreams and desires to come true.

NOVEMBER 19TH

Exodus 15:18—"The Lord reigns forever and ever."

God wants to rule and reign in your life! He doesn't want fear, anger, depression, loneliness, money, doubt, or you name it to rule you. God desires to be the one to reign and preside over your life. Are your situations ruling you, or are you letting God rule over your situations? God wants you to live in his strength. If there is something in your life that is controlling you, God has a way out!

THE TAKEAWAY: Are you allowing God to rule and reign over your life? Let him preside over all your affairs.

NOVEMBER 20TH

1 John 2:2—"He is the atoning sacrifice for our sins."

Atone isn't a word people use often. It means to make amends or to make something right. The problem is when we sin or make mistakes, we can never make things perfectly right on our own. We will drive ourselves crazy trying to do so. Are you attempting to make something right that only God can amend? The truth is Jesus has paid every single sin debt we owe when he died on the cross and rose from the grave.

THE TAKEAWAY: There is no replacement for the perfect sacrifice of Jesus. He restores, forgives, and heals perfectly.

NOVEMBER 21ST

Psalm 107:1—"Give thanks to the Lord, for he is good; his love endures forever."

Have you ever started to eat something but then noticed it was past the expiration date? Unfortunately, you had to throw the food away because it was no longer fresh. Can I give you some good news? There are no expiration dates with God and his promises. His love endures forever. Wow! The key is that God's love continues endlessly, never expiring. No matter what you have done or where you have gone, remember that "his love endures forever", and this is one promise that won't ever expire!

THE TAKEAWAY: Our life's focus needs to be on walking with God. Our relationship with God is the only thing we have now that we will have forever.

NOVEMBER 22ND

Psalm 107:6—"Then they cried out to the Lord in their trouble, and he delivered them from their distress."

Do you need to be rescued? Are you tired of the drama, the pains, the worries, or just the everyday struggles of life? Notice in this verse that God brings the answer to our cries for help in that "he" delivers us from our distress. I am convinced that so much of living this life is not so much about what I do, but what I let God do in my life. Let him rescue you from any of the troubles you may be facing today!

THE TAKEAWAY: There is so much about our lives that only God can heal. Don't try to do what only God can do. Our job is to cry out to him, and we can trust him to deliver us from our distress.

NOVEMBER 23RD

Romans 1:16—"For I am not ashamed of the gospel, because it is the power of God that brings salvation to everyone who believes."

Do you need the power of God in your life? Power to change, not to give up, to hang on, or the power to turn away from temptation and sin? God wants to give you his power, but the key is not to be ashamed of the gospel. Today, I want to encourage you not to be ashamed of God and not to be ashamed of whom God has made you. It might not be popular by the world's standards to serve God, but it sure is powerful to serve him.

THE TAKEAWAY: If you are fearful about what others think, you can never climb to the heights of all the blessings God has in store for you!

NOVEMBER 24TH

Psalm 108:4—"Your faithfulness reaches to the skies."

Isn't it great to have a friend you can trust? Doesn't it feel good to have someone in your life who has your back no matter what? Friend, God has extended his faithfulness to us. He is dependable when we aren't. If God has told you he will do something, he will do it. His promises to bless, heal, and protect you—found in the Bible—are trustworthy. There is an old hymn, "What a friend we have in Jesus" that serves as a great reminder of God's love and faithfulness to us.

THE TAKEAWAY: Those who trust themselves will always be disappointed. Those who trust God will always be more than satisfied!

NOVEMBER 25TH

Romans 2:11—"For God does not show favoritism."

Do you ever feel as if some people have all the favor and you don't? Sometimes we might ask God for something in prayer and when we don't receive an immediate answer, we start to think maybe he isn't listening. Then, when we see someone else receive what we wanted, we begin to think God might favor that person more than he favors us. However, God's delays are not God's denials. In other words, just because God hasn't answered your prayers in the way you hoped yet, doesn't mean he won't. He doesn't show favoritism because we are all his favorites!

THE TAKEAWAY: God's delays are not God's denials.

NOVEMBER 26TH

Romans 5:20—"But where sin increased, grace increased all the more."

God has an answer to the biggest problem we face, which is sin. Sin is what separates us from God and the blessed life. God's answer to our sin problem wasn't to give more judgment; God's answer to our sin problem was to give us grace. Not just grace, but abundant grace. Can you imagine if you owed a ten-dollar bill at a restaurant, and someone else paid off that bill with a million dollars? God has made an overpayment for our sins!

THE TAKEAWAY: The grace of God is for our sins in the past, present, and future.

NOVEMBER 27TH

Romans 6:23—"For the wages of sin is death, but the gift of God is eternal life in Christ Jesus our Lord."

Are you taking advantage of the gift God has given you? The gift I am talking about is life; so don't let it pass you by! If a part of your life is dead, or if you have a dream, vision, or desire that is on life support, grab a hold of this promise. God gives the gift of life, but we must accept his gift. He wants us to have eternal life through Jesus and he wants us to have an extraordinary life here on earth. Receive that gift today!

THE TAKEAWAY: Don't wait to start living. Step out in boldness! God will never empower you to be someone else. He will empower you to be who he wants you to be.

NOVEMBER 28TH

Joshua 1:5—"I will never leave you nor forsake you."

God demonstrates in today's verse that he is our perfect Father. I know the vast majority of fathers who read this love their children, but no father is perfect except for our Heavenly Father. It is amazing to understand this truth that no matter what we do or where we go, he will not leave or forsake us. The most loving earthly fathers are limited by time and space. However, God isn't limited and can be present with us all the time. No matter what you are facing, remember that you are never alone.

THE TAKEAWAY: Consider this thought today: every place you go, God is going with you!

NOVEMBER 29TH

2 Corinthians 5:1—"For we know that if the earthly tent we live in is destroyed, we have a building from God, an eternal house in heaven, not built by human hands."

I did part of a funeral for a 96-year-old woman of God one day. It was a celebration of her life on earth and eternal life with God. Have you heard the phrase, "Don't sweat the small stuff"? That phrase had more meaning to me after doing the funeral. For those whose faith is in Jesus, this life is but an appetizer of the true life that is to come. We all have stuff that could be fixed or changed, but what is truly most important isn't the temporary but the eternal. Today, don't sweat the small stuff.

THE TAKEAWAY: We make mistakes when we view life through the temporary eyes of man. We need to view life through the eternal eyes of God.

NOVEMBER 30TH

Psalm 127:1—"Unless the Lord builds the house, the builders labor in vain."

God wants to build a great life for us. If we choose to do things God's way, there can be challenging times, but he ensures that we will make it through those times. When we do things independently of God's will, we usually end up harming ourselves and don't really get anything accomplished. Furthermore, when we don't do things God's way, we always hurt others. If you are doing something God doesn't want you to do, stop wasting your time.

THE TAKEAWAY: When we do things God's way, there are no regrets. When we do things man's way, there will always be regrets.

DECEMBER 1ST

Lamentations 3:22-23—"For his compassions never fail. They are new every morning."

Doesn't fresh food taste good? Isn't it nice to go in to a freshly painted room? Do you enjoy the smell of a brand new car? For some reason, we as people love things new. In this verse, God promises to give us his compassion and mercy. But then notice the Bible goes on to say, "They are new every morning." God wants us to understand that every morning his mercy is fresh and new. What a great thought that God's love and compassion is new for us every day!

THE TAKEAWAY: Are you only talking about the things God did in the past? Thank God for what he did in the past, but God wants to do amazing things in our lives right now today.

DECEMBER 2ND

Psalm 118:13—"I was pushed back and about to fall, but the Lord helped me."

Do you feel as though you are being pushed back today in some area of your life? As believers in Jesus, God doesn't promise that we won't have moments where we will get pushed, but he does promise that we don't have to fall. Today, when you are almost pushed beyond your breaking point, know that God will come to your rescue and keep you from falling.

THE TAKEAWAY: Not only does God help us so we don't fall, but we can push the enemy back by choosing to praise God during those difficult times.

DECEMBER 3RD

Psalm 135:5—"Our Lord is greater than all gods."

Notice the Bible says our Lord is greater than all gods. He is greater than the god of money, than the god of fame, than the god of popularity, than any god that is man based and of this world. As you journey through life today, don't let anything stop you from God's very best for your life. Sometimes, we start serving others gods and may not even realize it. Make sure every part of your life is surrendered and focused on the Lord God Almighty!

THE TAKEAWAY: How can you tell if you are serving other gods? When the temporary things in this life have more of your attention than the eternal, you are serving a man-centered god.

DECEMBER 4TH

John 15:16—"You did not choose me, but I chose you."

We have to earn a lot of things in life. We have to earn a paycheck, respect, the right to be heard, a living, and sometimes even friendships. However, we do not need to earn God's love or approval. Sometimes, God does not approve of what we do, but he always loves us. Today, bask in what you didn't have to earn, God's love!

THE TAKEAWAY: If you want to change people's lives, do to them what God has done to you. If you give people love they don't deserve, you will change the world!

DECEMBER 5TH

Romans 8:1—"Therefore, there is now no condemnation for those who are in Christ Jesus."

Have you ever done something wrong and then couldn't stop feeling the shame from what you did? God makes an unbelievable promise that there is now no condemnation for those whose faith is in Christ. If you are feeling guilt-ridden for a mistake you made and you have already asked God to forgive you, those feelings aren't from God. God wants you to understand that you are forgiven! He doesn't want you to hold on to the pain from the past; this is not his will.

THE TAKEAWAY: Look at that often-missed word in today's verse, *now*. Once you turn to God, he removes all the guilt and condemnation right now!

DECEMBER 6TH

Psalm 139:14—"I praise you because I am fearfully and wonderfully made."

Today, it seems as though many people spend time trying to change things they don't like about themselves. How many people are on diets or have memberships to gyms? How many people spend hundreds or thousands of dollars on their outer appearance? Friend, God made you perfect just the way you are. Sure, there may be times when our attitude may need some adjusting, but God made you, and you are fearfully and wonderfully made!

THE TAKEAWAY: You are God's masterpiece!

DECEMBER 7TH

Romans 11:34—"Who has known the mind of the Lord? Or who has been his counselor?"

Do you need wise counsel today? It just takes one wrong choice to affect us and bring our lives pain. God wants to give you his wisdom today. Friend, don't try to make decisions alone. If you need wisdom about any area of your life, ask God and then listen for his response. My pastor once said, "If it is big enough to bother you, it is big enough to bring to God." Take all your big and little cares to God. He is a wonderful counselor and will give you his wisdom.

THE TAKEAWAY: Oftentimes, the devil will tell us not to bother God because the problem we are facing is so small. The heart of God eagerly wants us to bring all of our cares to him.

DECEMBER 8TH

Romans 12:21—"Do not be overcome by evil, but overcome evil with good."

You can't fight fire with fire. You can only fight fire with water. Is someone trying to cause you pain or harm? Perhaps a friend, spouse, family member, or coworker is pushing your buttons. The answer is not returning harm for harm but returning healing for harm. One of the most difficult things to do is treat someone with love who hasn't shown you love or kindness. If you want the problem to remain, give people what they deserve. If you want the problem fixed, give people what they don't deserve, God's love.

THE TAKEAWAY: If you fight fire with fire, everyone gets burned.

DECEMBER 9TH

Colossians 1:12—"The Father, who has qualified you to share in the inheritance."

Many people have experienced disappointment upon hearing the news they didn't get a job or promotion because they were not qualified. I want to give you good news today. With God, you are qualified! You are qualified to be blessed, healed, prosperous, filled with joy, do the impossible, have peace deep in your heart, have eternal life, and so much more. Why are you qualified? Because God's Son, Jesus, loves you so much that by his death and resurrection, he has qualified you. Isn't that amazing news?

THE TAKEAWAY: No power in hell can stop a believer who knows who he or she is in Christ.

DECEMBER 10TH

Isaiah 41:10—"So do not fear, for I am with you."

Have you ever been scared? It is fine to be temporarily scared. However, it is not reasonable to live a life of fear. God does not want fear to rule your life. He is an all-powerful, loving God who protects, heals, and guides those who call on his name. Today, if you are afraid of something small, such as a person's opinion about you, or something big such as cancer, God says you don't have to be scared. He is with you.

THE TAKEAWAY: Nothing can stop the supernatural miracle-working power of God in the life of a Christian like fear. Don't give into fear; give into faith!

DECEMBER 11TH

Psalm 145:13—"The Lord is trustworthy in all he promises."

I try to do everything I say I am going to do, but sometimes, I fall short in keeping my promises. On the other hand, God always keeps his promises to heal our lives, to forgive our sins, to give us favor, to love us uncondi- tionally, to give us peace of mind, and so much more. And with all those promises, he is faithful. He hasn't lost track of you, and he sure hasn't lost track of his promises. If you are waiting for an answer to a prayer or a promise God has given you, just hold on a little while longer. God is trustworthy!

THE TAKEAWAY: Waiting is not always an easy thing to do. The only thing worse than waiting, is giving up on God too soon, so don't give up!

DECEMBER 12TH

Psalm 146:7—"The Lord sets prisoners free."

Are you locked up today? Not in a jail cell but perhaps in a prison of guilt? Or, maybe imprisoned by fear or shame? Perhaps you find yourself in the prison of loneliness, depression, anxiety, doubt, or sin. Friend, God wants you to realize that because his Son Jesus died for you and rose from the grave, you are free! The keys of human intelligence, corporate bargaining, and leadership strategies can never unlock the chains of this life. The Lord is the hero of our lives and the only one who gives us true freedom.

THE TAKEAWAY: There is no substitute for what the Spirit of God can do. Freedom is found in living in God's ways. Bondage in life is found in living our lives without consulting God.

DECEMBER 13TH

1 Corinthians 2:5—"So that your faith might not rest on human wisdom, but on God's power."

Do you need godly counsel today? Spend time honestly listening to God. God has the power to change any issue or situation. There is nothing wrong with seeking counsel and wisdom from a family member or friend, but that person could unintentionally give you incorrect advice. Today, seek God's wisdom for your life. Put your faith in God's power and plans.

THE TAKEAWAY: Human effort will never accomplish what the Spirit of God can do. Do not allow yourself to substitute the ideas or powers of man for those of God.

DECEMBER 14TH

1 Corinthians 2:9—"What no eye has seen, what no ear has heard, and what no mind has conceived—the things God has prepared for those who love him."

Surprise! Have you ever attended or been a part of a surprise party? Watching my mom's reaction as we surprised her for a milestone birthday was such a great blessing for me. Friend, God has a wonderful surprise for us when we pass away…heaven! We can't fully understand how great it will be. Heaven will be so grand, so awe-inspiring, and so overwhelming; we just can't even come close to comprehending how amazing it will be.

THE TAKEAWAY: The most valuable resource you will see today is people. We want to do everything we can to bring every single person in our sphere of influence to a life-giving relationship with Jesus.

DECEMBER 15TH

Psalm 149:4—"For the Lord takes delight in his people."

It doesn't matter how intelligent you might be or how long you have been a Christian. Our understanding of how much God loves us just barely scratches the surface. The Bible says, "The Lord takes delight in his people." *Delight* means to take joy in. Do you know God takes joy in you? He loves you and you bring him joy. Just think: in spite of all our imperfections, we bring God joy because he delights in us.

THE TAKEAWAY: Today, think about this fact that God takes joy in you!

DECEMBER 16TH

Jeremiah 32:40—"I will never stop doing good to them."

Do you want some good news today? God's Word says, "I will never stop doing good to them." His Word does not say, "If my people are good, I will be good to them," or "If my people give money, I will be good to them." God's goodness to us is not based on our performance. God does not complete a performance review on our lives, and then determine to bless us. His Word says that he will never stop doing good to us.

THE TAKEAWAY: What part of *never* do you not understand?

DECEMBER 17TH

Proverbs 3:24—"When you lie down, your sleep will be sweet."

How well are you sleeping these days? God is interested in your sleeping and he wants your rest to be sweet. Unfortunately, many people don't sleep peacefully and find themselves tossing and turning throughout the night. One of the main reasons we don't sleep well is we carry burdens that God never intended for us to carry. Friend, give your burdens to our loving God who never slumbers, and start getting a good night's sleep!

THE TAKEAWAY: We can sleep sweetly because God is watching over us. We can sleep sweetly because God knows what we need. We can sleep sweetly because God is sovereign and isn't asleep on his job.

DECEMBER 18TH

Luke 1:37—"For no word from God will ever fail."

What would you like changed in your life that just doesn't seem possible? The good news is that nothing is impossible with God! Don't listen to those negative voices that say certain things in your life can never be turned around. Those are lies from the devil. God gives a promise that nothing is impossible, and when he says nothing, he means nothing. Oh, the joy we would have if we simply took God at his never failing Word!

THE TAKEAWAY: We need to believe God at his Word that with him, the impossible becomes possible!

DECEMBER 19TH

Psalm 103:2—"Forget not all his benefits."

Can you imagine receiving a $10,000 check and not cashing it? I have three words for you, cash the check! We do the same thing with God when we don't accept his love, peace, healing, strength, and power into our lives. Friend, God wants you to cash in on all the benefits he freely gives and for you to enjoy them in your life today.

THE TAKEAWAY: God is giving you benefits that you need to cash in on today while you still have time!

DECEMBER 20TH

Psalm 130:8—"He himself will redeem."

What if someone wrote you a $1,000 check and then stomped on it, kicked it, made a mark on it, and then crumpled it up. Could you still cash it? Yes! No matter what the check went through, the value wouldn't be damaged. Friend, no matter what you are going through today, you have great worth to God! God loves you, and you are valuable to him. He can redeem any situation in your life.

THE TAKEAWAY: Your value can never decrease as a child of God!

DECEMBER 21ST

Psalm 54:7—"You have delivered me from all my troubles."

David is the writer of this verse. God had used David to defeat a giant. However, that wasn't the biggest giant David had to face. The greatest enemy David had to face was himself. That same truth can be said of us. The only way we can overcome our poor choices or actions is by trusting God to deliver and repair brokenness in our lives. If we trust him, he will.

THE TAKEAWAY: The person who caused most of your problems is yourself. We need to make sure we are doing God's will and not our own.

DECEMBER 22ND

Proverbs 11:25—"A generous man will prosper; whoever refreshes others will be refreshed."

Listen to these wise sayings: "No man is emptier who is full of himself." "Money never made a man rich." Friend, if you want to have a full life, bless other people. Don't just bless them in a monetary way, but bless others by serving them when they are in need. Be a friend to those who don't have friends. Help someone who can't help him or herself. The more we love and serve others, the more we enjoy life.

THE TAKEAWAY: The only way to keep God's blessings is to give them away.

DECEMBER 23RD

Ezekiel 36:26—"I will give you a new heart and put a new spirit in you; I will remove from you your heart of stone and give you a heart of flesh."

Do you need a new heart? Has someone hurt you? Have you done something that has caused you sorrow? This verse says that God will give us a new heart. No matter who we are there will be times when our hearts get broken. God promises that no matter how bad our hearts get damaged, he can bring healing. Today, if someone or something has wounded you, let God do surgery on your heart.

THE TAKEAWAY: Only God can heal a broken heart.

DECEMBER 24TH

2 Corinthians 1:3—"The Father of compassion and the God of all comfort."

Are you facing adversity in your life today? Do you need relief from what is causing you pain? The Bible gives us this truth that God is the God of all comfort, which means he brings calm and healing to any situation you are facing. Today, share your concerns with God and receive his compassion and comfort. If you turn to anyone but God, the answer will only be a temporary fix.

THE TAKEAWAY: Hurting people hurt others. Healed people heal others.

DECEMBER 25TH

Matthew 1:21—"She will give birth to a son, and you are to give him the name Jesus, because he will save his people from their sins."

Merry Christmas! Friend, what makes Christmas merry is not just that a baby was born, but it is the fact that this baby became the Savior of the world. Jesus saved us from our sins, and he also rescues us from any other area of our lives that need to be saved. Does your marriage need to be saved? What about your money situation? What about a relationship? Or perhaps a dying dream that is in need of saving? Whatever you need saved, Jesus can do it. I pray you and yours have a Merry Christmas!

THE TAKEAWAY: Jesus came into a world of trouble to bring peace. Invite him into your world of trouble, and he will bring you peace.

DECEMBER 26TH

Proverbs 17:28—"Even fools are thought wise if they keep silent."

Friend, some of the best advice for our lives is to be silent! The next time your close friend or family member angers you, be quiet! The next time you are tempted to say something when you are impatient, be quiet! The next time you pray and ask God for help, be silent in his presence. Imagine how much power we would have in the Lord if we took more time to listen.

THE TAKEAWAY: Sometimes the wisest thing we can do is keep our mouths shut and be quick to listen.

DECEMBER 27TH

1 John 1:8—"If we claim to be without sin, we deceive ourselves and the truth is not in us."

Take the mask off. Nobody is perfect. Sometimes Christians try to appear as though they have it all together when in reality, they do not. Friend, God loves us so much; we can be real. We will all say, think, and do things at times that we are not proud of doing. The key is when we mess up, we need to be real with God and admit our mistakes. God loves us so much that we can take our masks off with him.

THE TAKEAWAY: Underneath your mask is a beautiful child of God!

DECEMBER 28TH

Nehemiah 8:10—"The Joy of the Lord is your strength."

Joy is a choice! Did you know that? This week, you can't choose how people are going to treat you. You can't choose what news is going to occur in your city or around the world. But you can choose your attitude. Today, I invite you to choose joy. The choice is up to you!

THE TAKEAWAY: Joy is a choice. What attitude are you going to choose today?

DECEMBER 29TH

Proverbs 21:31—"The horse is made ready for the day of battle, but victory rests with the Lord."

You aren't alone. Most times when I fail in life or make mistakes, it is because I try to go it alone. Friend, one piece of good news is that we don't have to go it alone in our marriages, in our money matters, in our families, or even in our death. This verse says there is victory with the Lord. Friend, God wants you to have his victory today.

THE TAKEAWAY: When you try to be the lone ranger in life, you will only end up hurting yourself and others. When you go with the Lord, he will give you victory.

DECEMBER 30TH

2 Corinthians 9:6—"Whoever sows sparingly will also reap sparingly."

God wants you blessed! However, in life, you get what you grow. Let me explain. If you plant the seeds of anger, lust, rudeness, greed, and selfishness, that is what will grow in your life. However, if you plant the seeds of grace, kindness, freely giving to others, and mercy, that is what you will reap. So, the point is to sow the seed in other people's lives that you want to reap in your life.

THE TAKEAWAY: You get what you grow. What are you allowing to cultivate in your heart?

DECEMBER 31ST

Proverbs 23:4—"Do not wear yourself out to get rich."

We are not given a great life or a terrible life. We are given life. It is up to us to determine what choices and paths we will follow. Seeking riches will always make you broke. There is nothing wrong with having money as long as money doesn't have you. If we seek God first, love others above ourselves, and do what God has called us to do we will be wealthy.

THE TAKEAWAY: The most important thing you can do with your life is to draw near to God and lead others to him!

Made in the USA
Columbia, SC
27 August 2018